Big Fat Lies

A story by Jamie Lopez

Layers

I walk through many lives
some of them my own
and I'm not who I was
through some principal of being
abides, from which I struggle
not to stray

When I look behind
as I am compelled to look
before I can gather strength
to proceed on my journey
I see the milestone dwindling
towards the horizon
the slow fire trailing
from the abandoned campsite
over which scavenger angles
wheels on heavy wings
Oh, I made myself a tribe
out of true affection
and my tribe is scattered
How shall the heart be reconciled
to the feast of losses?
In a rising wind

the manic dust of my friends
Those who fell along the way
bitterly stings my face
Yet I turn, I turn
exulting somewhat
The manic dust of my friends
those who fell along the way
bitterly stinging my face
Yet I turn, I turn
exulting somewhat
with my will intact to go
Wherever I need to go
and every stone on the road
precious to me
In my darkest night
When the moon was covered
and I roam through wreckage
a nimbus-clouded voice
directed me
Live in the layers
not on the liter
Though I lack the art
to decipher it.
No doubt the next chapter
in my book of transformations
is already written

For the reader...

This book is not a tell all. I'm not trying to throw people under the bus. I'm not trying to get revenge. Although it was something I thought about before, it's just not where my heart is today. I have to be accountable for my own actions. I was able to see the roles I played in a lot of situations I was in. I can admit that I keep people around who I know are users, especially men. Some of the same traits that my mom has that I hated all my life when it comes to men, I have. Through this process I realized that I'm beginning to do the same things. Every major downfall I ever had in my life always stemmed from me being depressed over a relationship with the wrong man. Even as I'm writing this book, I have the wrong man lying beside me. Someone who's here for the wrong reason. He doesn't really need me to financially take care of him like some of the others, but he is around for access. He wants to be a part of what I'm building. The difference between my mom and I is that she finds financially secure men and I find men who expect me to take care of them. This has been my downfall from the beginning of my story even to this day.

I'm still trying today to shake a man who I know is using me for an opportunity. He wants to be a part of the opportunity, but I need the attention. I crave it. I know it's not real. I know he doesn't love me, but what I've been through in the last few years, I need the attention. I know it sounds horrible, but I'm not perfect. I will no longer pretend to be perfect. I told myself I wasn't going to hide anything I'm going through anymore, because I want help. I want to be better. I know my triggers. I know I have a lot of things I need to fix about myself. This is my one big chance to really open up and tell the truth about my life. Past and present. My only goal is to have a better future. To heal. First, I had to learn to be truthful with myself. Then, I learned to stop creating a false narrative of what my life is. That's the hard part. I'm just trying to heal. I have been hurting so much for so long and I just want to stop the pain.

I want to heal physically, but more than anything I want to heal emotionally. It's the reason I chose this book cover. It looks glamorous and chaotic. It looks like I'm trying to cover up the truth with glitz and glamour and that's what I was doing. In this picture I was going to physical therapy and wasn't quite able to stand in the photo. A month later, I took a second photo, and I was able to stand. I was in so much pain in the photo and it showed on my face, because for the last few years I have been confined to my bed. Yes, you heard it right. I had gained so much weight I wasn't able to walk. That was one of my biggest secrets. The biggest part of my life I tried to hide. I told so many lies to cover up my truth.

At one time someone asked me if I was willing to die to keep this secret because they found it absurd how much effort I put into covering my truth. I told so many lies to cover up my reality instead of asking for help to live. I couldn't ask for help. I couldn't allow anyone to see how much pain I was in. I preach body positivity, but it was nothing positive about my life. At my biggest, I was over

800 pounds! I couldn't let anyone know. I had to cover up the truth. I couldn't let my community down. I wasn't thinking that my mental health was as messed up as my physical health was as I was willing to keep up a narrative to support a community that didn't really support me.

Everything I tried to do to help my community of plus size women had failed. Why? Because they didn't support me. No matter how hard I had to fight, I was still willing to lie to the world and almost die because I had to continue to fight for my community. That's what I promised my mentor who had passed away. She too had given her all to a community that wasn't there when she died after being bed-ridden because of her weight. I almost had her fate because the life that I perpetuated on Instagram wasn't how it really was.

There was a time that I was willing to die to keep me being dangerously overweight a secret. I couldn't ask for her help because I would be exposing myself. It took me almost dying to realize I was done living a fake life. I want to really live. This picture is so important because for months I have been working with a physical therapist to learn how to walk again. My legs are still wobbly. I lost a lot of weight but I'm still terrified to walk on my own. My fear is that I will fall and not have anyone there to pick me up. Take a close look at my face in the picture I chose as my book cover. YOU SEE THE PAIN. You see how determined I am. You see how much I'm straining and fighting to not fall. It's ironic because I feel like I've been fighting not to fall for a long time, and I fell hard. This time around I'm fighting not to fall for all the right reasons.

All my health problems started with my mental health first and foremost. To heal my body, I have to heal my mind. This is my first step by telling my story. I am working through everything I have pinned up inside me. I apologize to everyone I ever hurt, took advantage of or pushed away. To protect a lot of my secrets I wasn't always emotionally available. My depression and anxiety were never being treated so instead I thought trying to be an overachiever would take away my sadness or would calm the anxious feeling that I felt all the time. I pushed away good people that help me build my dream and when it didn't work, I went my separate ways without even saying thank you sometimes. I lost some really good friends.

There were so many people that
even relocated to Las Vegas just to be a
part of me building Baby doll and if I
never said thank you, I would like to thank
you and apologize if I ever made you feel
like I wasn't grateful.

I've lost so many great friends on this journey. I was in a horrible emotional space when I started the journey. I was in denial of my mental health after my heartbreak. I thought that if the salon would be successful, it would heal me and all that I was fighting emotionally. That one day, the anxiety would just go away, but real success never came. I had the popularity now, but I was never able to really build the business the way I wanted. The lack of success never came like I wanted to and because of that the depression and anxiety only grew until it not only started to affect me mentally but physically. I wasn't ready to share that with the world. Those secrets that I kept almost killed me, but I made it through, and I am finally ready to heal. I have a hard road ahead of me.

There were the not-so-great people I had in my life. The people who used me for their own gain, the ones who were toxic and the ones I might have gravitated to the most because for some reason, I give the people who treat me bad way more chances than I give the ones who treat me good. I don't know why I do that, but I do. Something inside of me is drawn to pain, hurt, and confusion. Every man I have ever picked to be in my life was a user. Does that say something about them? Does that say something about me? I plan to dig deep in my healing process and try to heal. To start my healing process, I must start first by forgiving. So, I forgave anyone who had ever caused me any pain. I want to be free. I no longer want to hold resentment in my heart, I just want to live.

For the last couple of years, I have been fighting for my life and I'm still here. As I move on, I don't want to hold on to the things of the past. I forgive everyone who has wronged me, and I apologize to anyone that I have wronged. This is not an easy process. I'm not a perfect person, but I'm trying to be a better me. I have to heal physically and mentally all at the same time. I have been through so much or should I say I put myself through so much. As I dug deep, I realized that if I would have gotten help earlier on for my emotional scars, I may not have gone through all the things I went through physically. All I know is that I really want to start living my life. I haven't really lived a good life. I've been acting like I was happy for a long time. I dream of really being happy and I want to be healthy. I want to laugh and hang out with friends. I want to find love. I mean, real true love. I have limited myself for years.

Every day is a new adventure. I'm also in the process of healing physically. I kept a lot from the world but the last few years I haven't been able to get out of my bed. I came off a facade to impress the movement so much that I almost lost my life. Everyday I'm learning how to take a few steps and learning how to walk again. I'm learning to eat right, losing weight so I can live again. I refuse to lay down and die. I refuse to hide my pain and play make believe like my life is perfect. I'm in the season of healing. I want to have a real life. I don't want to be depressed. I'm tired of being scared that if I go to sleep, I may not wake up again. I don't want to be treated badly by men. I pick men that I know that's only using me. Something inside me lacks confidence or maybe I am just tired of being lonely. I want to mend old friendships with people that I wronged because of me trying to cover up what really was going on in my life. I don't want to lay in my bed all day and let life pass me by anymore.

I don't want to try to run my business from my bed and blame other people for not wanting to be a part of it. I feel sorry for the people who went broke trying to keep my salon doors open. I know I seemed ungrateful, but I was just hiding my pain. I expected so much from people who didn't owe me anything. I just want a second chance. God has kept me here for a reason. I want to be able to take a walk by myself. I want to be able to travel and sit on the beach all day. I want a tan and I want to dance and sing. I just want a normal life. I want to have fun. So, if I could ask 2 things from anyone reading this, I would ask that you please pray for me on my journey and please don't judge me in my process. Sometimes I may go back to some of my negative ways but just know I'm trying hard every day to become a better person. I'm not perfect. I'm no longer trying to portray a perfect life. I'm just going to try every day to get better and pray that one day I can just live a normal life. I don't want to live my life for the plus size movement. I don't want to try to live my life for a man and I'm not going to try to live my life for likes on an app. I'm going to live my life for myself one day at a time.

The Jamie Lopez Story

I want to start this book off by addressing my younger followers. The young, overweight girl who is trying to figure out life. The young woman looking for a place to fit in who may have landed on my page because she started to follow in my footsteps and enter the body positivity world. From looking down my timeline you may have started to attend some of the events I used to frequent. Maybe befriend some of the friends you saw on my timeline. You like my pictures and daydream about my flashy and fabulous life. I want to take the time to sit you down and tell you what I wish someone had told me before I began my journey of trying to find myself and my tribe. I want you to know everything that glitters ain't gold. I'm not only writing this book to heal, I'm writing it so my young followers won't make some of the same mistakes I have.

First of all, I want to be totally transparent with you. My life is not fabulous. It may look like it on social media, but a picture tells a thousand words. Take a closer look. I mean, really look at not just my pictures but other people you follow on social media. A lot of us are hiding pain behind a big smile, flashy new car, or a brand new over-priced purse. Yes, I'm a collector of beautiful things. For a longtime these things made me feel validated. Seeing people gravitate to things I liked made me feel seen and appreciated.

In the beginning it was to inspire and encourage girls like myself. Somehow, it all began to fall apart, and I started creating this false narrative by doing whatever I had to do to create this illusion that I had this happy, positive, and fabulous life. It was all a lie that almost sent me to my grave. My mind was so messed up with trying to keep up the lie, that I attracted some of the most negative and toxic people that helped cause me to crash and burn. I didn't know at the time, but I was surrounding myself around the wrong people. If I had only been honest with some of the things I was going through with my audience, things would probably never gotten as bad as they did. Any positive person that came into my life that really wanted to help was pushed away. I told so many lies, I couldn't let them see that I was attracted to the people who would only try to destroy me in the end. The users and abusers. Why did they feed me all the bullshit I needed to hear so they could get what they needed from me to keep my secrets?

It's a very ugly side to the body positivity movement and to know myself and my business had a lot to do with leading women into a movement that could be damaging and unrealistic that breaks my heart. I'm going to right my wrongs of helping to lead them to a toxic, and for some a mental and physically unhealthy lifestyle. I will start off by telling my real story. I know I'm going to get a lot of hate from telling the truth, but I'm also going to save some lives and that is all that matters.

I was left for dead and robbed for almost everything I owned, and I refuse to let that happen to anyone one else. I was broke pushing this false narrative like I was rich. It was all a lie. My business fell apart. I wasn't marketing to everyone. I was focusing on my tribe. That was a huge mistake because my tribe didn't support me. My intention was to never exclude anyone, but I had the wrong people around me and I let them turn my brand into something I never wanted. My goal is to include everyone and make everyone feel comfortable.

My advice to my young babydoll's is never let anyone put you in a box. Do not attach yourself to a bunch of hurt, plus size women, who just want to hurt and exclude other people only because they have been hurt in the past. Remember, body positive movement is supposed to lift people up, not put them down. I got caught up with a group of women who hated anyone who didn't mirror their image. A bunch of hurt people push their hate on other vulnerable women. I didn't see it at the time, but I see now that that was discrimination, and I will never be a part of putting another group of people down to make myself feel good.

I had some evil people around me and I had no idea because I was so naive at the time. I had aligned myself with some really negative people. At the time, I thought I had found what I have always been looking for. I never want this to happen to another Babydoll. I promise to create a safe space where everyone will feel safe. I promise to pay very close attention as we grow to make sure this brand is to lift people up. I want to pay the most attention to my young ladies who are at a vulnerable stage in life.

I don't know why we hurt ourselves to
please someone else's perception of self?
I'm sorry to my own reflection
I'm sorry for putting you down
I'm sorry I struggled accepting the beauty
that lies in myself
I am Sensitive
I am Emotional
I am Venerable
I am Strong

I am Passionate

I am Devoted

I am Growing

I am Grounded

I am a Lover

I am Fearless

I am confident

I am Me

I am letting go of Masks

I'm letting go of perfectionism

I'm sorry for covering your imperfections

I'm sorry for hiding your scars

I'm sorry that I put you down

But I'm willing to let you be known

I'm will to let you free knowing

This is my redemption. This is the

beginning.

2020

2020 was a horrible year for us all and the world felt like it was coming to an end. Many lost their lives and although I felt as if it was the end for me, I'm still here. I'm so thankful. Covid 19 was the scariest thing ever with all my health issues. I probably wouldn't have been able to survive if I had contracted the disease. Although I didn't contract the virus, I got sick in the middle of the most devastating time in history. It was the most difficult time for me. I was scared and my family was hundreds of miles away.

Try getting sick in the middle of a world disaster! I had been sick for a long time, but my body had taken all that it could take. While the world was trying to heal, my heart was failing, and it was one of the scariest times of my life. If it wasn't for one of my castmates secretly calling the ambulance, I most likely wouldn't have made it. I was furious with her at the time because I hated hospitals. She didn't care or maybe I should say she did care. She recognized I had some of the same symptoms as her father that had heart issues. She was right. Nothing that I say or do could show how much I appreciate her. She saved my life. I would like to thank her because if it wasn't for her, I would have died. I was all alone and in total denial of my health issues.

I remember like it was yesterday. We had just wrapped shooting our reality show and because of the virus, the world was shutting down. The production company had just announced that we were pausing production. I was happy because

I wasn't feeling my best, but I had gotten used to being sick. I suffered in silence. I would gather up the strength during production and as soon as production would end, I would go back to an unhealthy lifestyle. That unhealthy lifestyle almost cost me my life. There was no one there to really see what was going on. The fake happy Facebook post and the recycled pictures had become a part of my lifestyle. Most of the time, I would be in my bed rotting away. I was hiding from the world. Telling a false story of happiness but I was really suffering. My castmate called the ambulance that day without my knowledge. I must've looked sicker than I thought. I hit rock bottom right before I could start on my healing process. Today I'm much better. I'm in therapy and begin to walk again. I don't wish to being bedridden with anyone in the world. It doesn't only mess with your health, but it messes with your mind. If there are any of my dolls going through this, I'm there with you. I want to take the time to send you love and life. It's a whole world out there we have to see. We have to fight together. Forget everything I said in the past about this whole body positive movement. If you are at the point that your weight is affecting your health, it's nothing positive about that. Nothing is worth your health. I let what people may think about me take over my life. I was so busy trying to cover up how much my health was declining because of my weight.

To explain to you how hard this process has been I have to take it back. I have always been a big girl, but trauma is what got me to the point that I almost lost my life. It was like one day I had so much pain inside. So many unresolved issues. I just wanted to be in my own little world. I set up my life to where I never really had to leave home. Yes, I had a business, but I could run it from home. Technology was a gift and a curse for me. I could watch my salon on cameras. I had a second job where I worked from home. I could do my glam from home. I could order my groceries from home. I could make friends on the internet and show them these gorgeous pictures, lavish items, and build this image the whole world would love without them getting close to see I was really damaged and hurt.

As my team and I completed this book, this is literally one of the hardest things I have done other than fighting for my life the last few years. Come to think of it, I think of this also as a part of fighting for my life. It's actually one of the biggest pieces of the puzzle. I'm healing something that led me in the dark path in the first place. My mental health. Yes, I probably should talk to a therapist. I actually tried that, but I believe as people we all heal in different ways. For me telling my real story is the only way I'm going to heal. I held so much in for so long. I told so many lies to cover all the hurt and trauma I was experiencing. It was a never ending story. One little white lie turned into endless lies. In my defense, a lot of the lies I told were to protect the brand. I was determined to continue my mission.

What I didn't understand at the time was that the people I was trying to help didn't give a damn about me. I always heard about different women empowerment groups turning into more of a scene from Mean Girls. I didn't realize how much it was happening in the plus size community. In the beginning, once again, I was naive. Doll I know you're a little confused. You may have thought I built the BABYDOLL brand on being transparent. That wasn't exactly true. The truth was most of it was a lie, but it didn't start out that way. I built this business to help women like myself who have been discriminated against in the beauty industry. I wanted to create a safe space where we didn't let the rest of the world define our definition of beautiful. In the mix of me trying to help a whole movement of BBW women, I lost myself and once I lost myself all shit hit the fan. I was trying to be the face and a warrior for a whole community that left me for dead.

My decision to tell my true story is for a few different reasons. The first reason is that it may be someone somewhere going through a lot of the things I just went through. I want to give you a little advice. Never let a group, movement, business, or group of friends make you jeopardize yourself to please them. You can't live your life to please other people. The second reason I decided to tell my story was because for years I let people hold my story over my head. They threatened to tell my secrets. Things that I hid from everyone including my mental stability and my health issues is what they threatened to expose me with. I couldn't let that happen so for years I kept people around who were toxic around me. I lied and schemed just to keep a secret that really wasn't a secret.

If someone just took a close look, they could see my life was spiraling. I mean damn, in most of my pictures I was sitting down or on a scooter. It wasn't hard to see that I could barely walk. My secret was to keep them distracted with all the beautiful things around me. People should talk to a therapist. I am working one day at a time to try to figure out what is best for me. I know things aren't the best in my life right now but I'm trying. This last year, I had been healing and trying my hardest to lose weight by working out and eating right. I worked with a physical therapist to learn how that works. When writing this book, I realized a few things. A lot of things people have been saying about me are true.

There are also a lot of lies out there about me. I'm here to set the record straight. I can start this book by creating this narrative about making people feel sorry for me but that's what got me here in the first place. I had a hand in creating one of the most selfish communities ever. A community that would later turn their backs on me. I'm not sure if I could even be mad at the community, because I had a hand in all of it. It wasn't all my fault and I'm damn sure not going to take it, but I'm going to own my part. I will say that I may have helped create a monster, but it wasn't my intention. My intention was to create a safe space for plus size women. While standing on my soapbox preaching for us to not be discriminated against, I also fueled a fire by playing the victim.

I didn't know this at the time but playing the victim would eventually be my biggest strength and eventually my biggest downfall. How is that? WELL, LET ME EXPLAIN quickly. Talking about my real life experience was one hundred percent genuine, but once I started to go viral I wasn't completely honest. Yes, I was discriminated against as a plus size woman, but not a lot of times. It wasn't intentional. Was it the salon's fault that my chain broke when I was paying to get a service done? No but I used my heart and embarrassment to level my next move. Yes, I wanted to help. I never wanted another plus size woman to ever feel like I felt that day. I wanted to create a solution and I did. I'm very proud of that, but where I went wrong was not healing emotionally.

Without even knowing it because of me being fueled from pain and eventually hate I helped birth a them vs us community by mistake. It's not until I got sick, and I mean really sick, that I realized that I was one of the leaders of a "Mean Girl" community hiding behind body positivity. All because somehow, I'm good at pretending. I'm good at the happily ever after but really the happily ever after is literally just something I made up in my head. I pretended things have been good so long when they have been nothing short of a disaster. I've always been good with making things look good on the outside when things are a total disaster on the inside. It's like I cover my life up with a beautiful pink bandage.

Every person, place, or thing I let get close enough to try to pull the curtain back has always become a threat to me. I'm Jamie Lopez and this is my story. This story has actually been nothing but a disaster, but you would never know that because I made it look. I'm no longer a victim. I'm owning my shit and I want you all to own yours too! NO COMMUNITY IS GOING TO MAKE YOU LOVE YOURSELF. THAT HAS TO START WITH YOU! There's nothing wrong with having the support and guidance of a community but don't let anyone take you down a negative path. The big question is can this body positive community be fixed? The answer is ABSOLUTELY! It starts with fixing ourselves.

Body positivity is supposed to be about loving the skin you're in. If you let yourself get too big, you can't get around not loving yourself. If your weight is causing your health issues you can't be loving yourself. I know this is hard to hear dolls, but I'm telling you all this because I want to save some of you from going through what I've been through in the last year. I love all my dolls and I want to tell y'all what I wish someone told me. Let's really practice self-love. We can do this together.

Old Hollywood Glam

Since I was a young girl in grade school, I was always told I live in a fantasy world. My teachers were always calling my mom because I would show up in her makeup and jewelry. I felt like I was stuck in a life that I didn't belong to and until I got the life, I saw for myself I would pretend. It wasn't as bad when I was young unless I went overboard trying to dress or look too old for my age. The big problem was the older I got the bigger my imagination became. While most kids were starting to have a real life, I was still living in my own fantasy world which embarrassed my parents. I THINK if I was smaller, it wouldn't be such a big idea.

The fact of the matter was that I was almost 300 pounds in Junior High and that I already was an embarrassment to both my parents. Knowing I was big, and I was flashy annoyed my mom who was a beauty and it caused my dad to stay away. He would always say the world wasn't ready for a fat girl which drove me crazy because I got my weight from his side of the family. Now that I think of it, I think his embarrassment for me was about something deeper from his past, but we will get into that later.

Ever since I was a little girl, I gravitated to Hollywood glam, but not just any type of Hollywood glam. For me, it was the Old Hollywood that had a hold on me. All the glitz and glam had always done something to me. I always knew I was destined to be a star, and I was going to do it regardless of my size. I may have been plus size but everywhere I went I was going to be the flyest, most well put together girl in the room. I began to study the great s and I fell in love with Marilyn Monroe which was a puzzle to most. Here I was a plus size Latina girl and my idol was a white woman. Why wasn't it a Latina woman? It was something that people still bring up today. Well, it's simple, I am a girl who grew up in California in the valley. I was only surrounded by blonde hair, blue eyed girls. Growing up where most people looked the same, the definition of beauty was those types of girls.

Let me be clear: I am not and in no way ashamed of being a Puerto Rican girl. I just didn't know many Spanish women. Since growing older, I have found that

Spanish women are some of the most beautiful women on earth. The more I learn about my culture, the more I see what I missed out on as a child. I didn't have grandparents and I only knew my family that was in California. I never really knew another Puerto Rican family. I grew up in California. I grew up in the state of beauty and back then where I grew up it was nothing but blonde bombshells.

Remember, I was also living in a fantasy world and in my own little world, I was a part of Old Hollywood. Marilyn Monroe was my mentor and every day I would transform into being just like Marilyn. It wasn't only the image that made me fall in love with MARILYN Monroe, let me make that clear. I admit that's what it was at first and I don't know how many people knew this, but Marilyn was a plus size girl. She was a size 14 in a size 2 industry. Her rough upbringing, battle with depression, and anxiety was something I could relate to but what I could relate to the most was her glamour. It was how she developed a character that people would emulate for the years to come. What I didn't know was that every woman that spent most of their time trying to channel their inner Ms. Monroe was only manifesting a glamorous lifestyle.

Sometimes by trying to be so much like another person can cause you to develop their bad habits as well. I didn't see that at the time but a person who knew as much about Marilyn as I did should have known better than to channel Marilyn Monroe. Changing your whole image and personality to become someone else might not be the best thing to do. You're not only manifesting their looks and personality, you may also start to develop emotional problems or bad habits.

Anyone who knows anything about Marilyn, knows she had emotional and mental issues. I'm not saying I channeled all her emotional Issues because I already had my own battle. I used to compare my mental health with hers or maybe I was trying to be like her so much. Anyone who wants to be so much like a person with mental health issues but already had their own problems to start with, can be a recipe for disaster. I understand that now and although I still love Marilyn Monroe very much that's exactly why I'm writing this book to unpack all of my baggage.

I can think of another very successful but tragic life. Anna Nicole. The reason why she came to mind is she was the definition of someone who 100 percent mimicked Marilyn's life. Yes, it gave her some success, but it also caused her a lot of pain. Just thinking about her story and about how much she wanted to be exactly like Marilyn only to have her life spiral in the exact same way as Marilyn's life. It was so similar it was scary.

I will mostly always be a fan of Old Hollywood. Yes, and now I can admit to myself that I spent most of my life fantasizing about the life I wanted to live without actually doing much to live the life I want to live. Yes, I started my dream salon and everything but I got stuck in making things look good on the outside when they were really falling apart on the inside. My business has never turned a profit. Let's start there. I put more money in the business but never made one dime. Now I'm saying it out loud and even admitting it to myself. I'm ashamed. I'm ashamed because instead of covering up my failures, I could have asked for help. I did reach out to a few people for help but the minute they started to see through the illusion and lies, I had to distance myself. I couldn't let anyone know that I was hanging on by a string when it came to my business, my personal life, and more than anything my emotional well-being. My mental health was in a horrible state. This is something I'm still dealing with. Yes, the weight was an issue, but it all started with my mental state. Depression and social anxiety took over my life and because of it my health deteriorated quickly.

Letter to My Parents

I just want to be wonderful despite my abusive, neglected childhood. I never let it make me bitter. At least, that's what I told myself and that was a lie. My relationship made me super bitter. I always felt like I was looking for acceptance. I had my siblings but deep down I was always a little resentful of them because of the way my mother treated me. If it wasn't for music, beauty, and fashion I don't know where I would be. I remember winning my very first talent shows in the 4th grade. I sang Mariah Carey's Heroes. I was so emotional. It was something about the lyrics. They were powerful. I was crying out and I didn't even realize it at the time.

I needed a Hero. I needed someone to show me the love I wanted from my parents. I never felt loved by either of my parents.

I believe my appearance was an embarrassment to both of them. They hated the way I looked. All I ever heard from both of my parents for most part of my life was how I needed to fix my appearance. This confused me because I always made sure I looked my best. I have always been well put together. Always been glamorous because in my head I was channeling my inner Marilyn Monroe. To them my perfect makeup, well put together outfits, and name brand accessories wasn't enough. I was fat and in the words of my father, "the world wasn't ready for a fat girl."

No matter how beautiful my features were to them, the genes that they gave me were a whole big waste because I was fat. Their beautiful baby girl would only be nothing but pretty for a fat girl in their eyes. If only I could lose weight, I would fit into their perfect image of what they wished I was. What they didn't understand is the more they showed me how embarrassed they were of me, the more I drifted into depression. The depression just caused me to eat more and more. Food was my comfort. The bigger I got, the more our relationship went downhill until it was eventually almost non-existent. I was still a child. This happened at an early age. I've been a lonely girl for a long time. I'm realizing through writing this book that I'm still the same lonely little girl who used to have conversations with my parents about my weight. The disappointed and judgmental looks on their face still haunt me almost 20 plus years later. Realizing this, honestly the thought of this hurts but in order for me to heal I have to revisit all my pain.

Meet the Parents

9/11/2018

Dear Dad,

I forgive you and all the broken promises,
all the neglect, abuse, and all the lies. I
know you loved me to the best of your
ability. Hope I make you proud especially
because you told me the world wasn't
ready for a big girl.

Love,

Jamie

I wrote this letter to my dad on
9/11/ 2018. He had already passed away,
but I needed to write this for myself. For
me it was about getting the feelings out

and healing. In order for me to see where a lot of my pain and poor decision making came from, I had to go all the way back. All of my pain started from my relationship with my parents. Both very different but both extremely toxic. It's so sad because I loved them both so much. When I was younger, I dreamed of my dad taking me from my mother's household. It wasn't that I didn't love my mom, I loved her dearly, but we just didn't get alone. I felt like she would put her relationships with men before me. What I didn't realize was that my relationship with my dad was mostly a fantasy. Something I made up in my head.

With my father, I would have most likely fit in his life more if I was thin. It was all about the image with him which was weird because he wasn't a small man.

Everyone on his side of the family was big so I had his genes. I guess my father hated me. I didn't really know much about his family. The picture he showed me pretty much told the story of my family tree. I wish I would have met his family then I would have understood him more. Sometimes, I wonder if my mom was a secret. She was still a teenager when she met him. Maybe he kept his Hollywood life separate from his real life. It was something a lot of people did. Still at a young age, I thought my life would be amazing if I was just able to live with my dad. His confidence and flashy presents were intoxicating, and I was beyond hooked. Now, I see where I got it from. Now, I wonder if he was trying to hide his insecurities with flashy things the same way I did. I wish he was here. I have so many questions.

I dreamed that if I lived with my dad, I would have this beautiful, glamorous life. I always had this vivid imagination and to me at a young age my dad was important, wealthy, and flashy. The type of life he lived was the life I was destined to live. For a long time, my dream was to live with my dad. I always prayed that he would tell my mother he thought it was best I lived with him. My dad was a flashy man who loved money, glamorous younger women, and flashy cars. I think that's one of the reasons I tried to live a glamorous lifestyle. Even if it was messed up, it looked beautiful on the outside. I'm reasonably realizing a lot of my thought process came from my father. He was the definition of the California Lifestyle.

He worked hard and partied harder. During the day he was this hardworking, important lawyer. At night, he was this play boy who loved beautiful young women and had the California life most dreamt about. I was infatuated with him. Before I knew any better, I thought he was everything a man should be. His life was something that captivated me. I knew it was a lifestyle I was meant to be a part of, but he wouldn't have me. I didn't fit. The world wasn't ready for a fat girl, was what he would tell me. Those words still haunt me.

My younger memories of my dad weren't always pleasant. I remember waiting for him to come and get me. Sometimes he would show up and sometimes he wouldn't. When he did, I remember my mom wanting everything to be perfect. Most of the time we would always meet him somewhere. My mom would make sure we both were looking our best. I was always excited. She was just as excited, although she would never admit it. Their relationship was always a mystery to me. I know my mom had left home and was pretty much on her own as a teenager. My father was an older man and from my knowledge he always helped take care of her. I still don't quite understand.

My dad was 38 years old, and my mom was 17 when she got pregnant with me. I don't know how long he was dating her before she got pregnant but what would make a 38 year old man want to be with a girl that young? I guess it was the 80's and the times were different, but I just have so many questions.

My mom was always happy to see him, so I don't think he took advantage of her. The relationship was always a mystery to me. Maybe I will ask her one day. I will save that for the next book. The only time I really ever saw them have an argument was over me. My dad would be furious about my weight, chastising my mom for letting me get so big. My mom would be embarrassed and disappointed. She put in so much work to make me look pretty for our visits. Now that I look back, she needed his approval just as much as I did. Maybe he was controlling her with money. She had already been with my step father so I don't think she was still in love with him although they flirted a lot. Maybe this visit was necessary for her to get him to financially support me. It was like she wanted to prove to him how well she was taking care of me. The visits were never really fun. I always felt like I was on display. No matter how pretty my dress was or how nice my mom did my hair it was never good enough for my dad. I was overweight. What he wanted most was for me to be skinner. After the visit was over and we left I always felt horrible. I felt the disappointment and resentment from my mom without her even saying one word. Both of us wanted to please a man that couldn't be pleased. His lifestyle was the 80s California lifestyle. He wanted everything to be perfect and I didn't fit in his world. Now you see where I get this fairytale life from? I was born into it. Everything looks good on the outside but is horrible in real life. I picked up a lot of my father's traits without really being around him. I think I fell in love with his flashy living more than him. It had to be because I barely knew him. All I knew was that he was important and had an amazing life without me. As I got older the visits were less frequent and for a while, I didn't see him at all. By this time my mom had gotten married and started having more kids with her husband. I felt like an outcast. I'm not sure if my dad was helping to support me in his absence, but I don't think so. My mom was no longer giddy when she spoke his name; she only complained. When I got to my teenage years, she was over having me be a part of her perfect family. She said I was too much to handle. I was in too much trouble. Our relationship was in a horrible space. I prayed day and night for my dad to come let me live with him but that never happened. He did let me in his life shortly but that only ended in a disaster.

In 2009 my dad died. When he died, we weren't even speaking. We had connected some years back. I was excited. I had just graduated from the Job Corps and didn't have anywhere to go. I had been estranged from my family for a few years and I was excited to mend our relationship. I forgave him for not coming for me when my mom sent me to the group home. I was lonely and needed a connection with my family. My mom had put me in a group home when I was just a teenager, and she never came back for me. After I left the group home, I went to the Job Corps. When I graduated, I reconnected with my father and I was so happy. I finally had a place in his life. He finally stepped up when my mom abandoned me. At least that's what I felt like she did. The last few years I was in the group home and the Job Corps, I didn't have any contact with any of my family. I was pretty much on my own so when my dad reached out, I was overjoyed.

I thought that just maybe I could have the relationship with him I prayed for all of my life. He was apologetic that I had been abandoned. He promised me he would make it right and I was hopeful. As far as I was concerned, I was done with my mother and stepfather. They didn't care about me, and I was over trying to be a part of a family that they didn't want me to be a part of. My mom had this new family with my stepfather and their kids, and I didn't fit in. Nothing about me fit in. I had come to terms with that, and I was ready to create a life for myself. I didn't plan to have my dad around because he didn't show up at all when my mom put me in the group home, but I was willing to forgive. I was lonely and scared but having him in my corner for my new chapter in life was what I had prayed for. At least, that's what I thought. This wasn't the happily ever after I prayed for. My dad had an ulterior motive.

The day my dad reached out to me I was so excited. I had no idea what I would do after the Job Corp. It had been a few years and I had little to no contact with either of my parents. My mom just dropped me off at a group home and after I was 18 I went directly to the Job Corp. I wasn't exactly prepared for the real world after I graduated so the chance to live the life with my father was what I had always dreamed of. It was something I had prayed for every day. I had no idea he had ulterior motives. I mean, I was his little girl in my head. I thought that he just felt guilty for all I had been through in the last few years.

I did not question him as to why he didn't come for me sooner. I didn't want to offend him. I knew if I asked a question, it may cause him to change his mind, so I did whatever he needed me to do to make the relationship right. Now that I look back, I realize this behavior would follow me the rest of my life with every man I dated. I would continue my life trying to cater to a man who didn't really want to be bothered with me. I would do whatever I could to keep them in my life, disregarding how they made me feel. My only goal was to keep them in my life anyway I could. I learned this behavior from my relationship with my father. They say your dad is the first man that a girl falls in love with.

A girl's relationship with her dad will follow her into womanhood. The relationship with my dad was toxic and because of my relationship with him every man I ever dated was toxic. I mean really toxic. I never felt good enough for anyone and I was always trying to figure out what I could do or give them to keep them around, but we will get into that a little later.

When my dad came to get me, he told me he would put me in a comfortable apartment. I knew he had good taste, so I was overjoyed that everything was falling into place. I really had high hopes. He wanted me to prepare for the real world, is what he would always tell me. I was ready!!! The agreement was he would pay all my bills, but he needed me to take out a business account in my name. I didn't think about it at the time. I knew my dad was a legit businessman so anything he needed me for concerning his firm, I was willing to do. I wanted him to see I had some value. It didn't seem strange to me, but now that I think about it I have so many questions. What grown man who was a lawyer needed his barely adult daughter to get business accounts in her name? After all the years of being a successful Hollywood Lawyer, why could he not get the business account in his own name? He did eventually put his name on the account but not right away. Was he doing something illegal? Was he so fucked up that he was willing to put his own daughter in jeopardy? Was he hiding money for someone? I have so many questions that I would never be able to ask him because he is no longer here.

Now being a businesswoman, I realize that something was up. I know my dad had a spending problem and the young women he dated who were only a few years older than me lived lavish lifestyles. Maybe he had money problems trying to keep up in Hollywood with women half his age. Maybe the confident man I thought my father was, wasn't exactly true. Maybe just like myself he was chasing a lifestyle he couldn't really afford. Without even noticing or really knowing, everything he went through in life my life became very similar to his.

My relationship with my dad didn't last long after he got me in the apartment, and I got the bank accounts in my name. I mean at first things were great. He did everything he promised he would do. He made sure he paid all my bills, and we were on great terms. I felt like I was at the top of the world. At this time, I hadn't really mended everything with my mom but at least we were on speaking terms. She always had something to say about my father which offended me. I mean how could she have an opinion when she put me in a group home and left me there because of her husband and new family? So, to me she was just jealous that someone was finally showing me some love.

At the time, my father and I were in an amazing place, and I wasn't about to let anyone come in between that. My mom's criticism and warnings fell on deaf ears. If I could have just put some of the ill feelings I had towards her to the side, I would've realized that some of her concerns were valid. But again, how could she have anything to say after what she had done to me and at the time me and my father's relationship was great? I didn't get to see him as much as I liked but when we spoke, he made me feel important, especially since I had the account in my name. I felt as though I was contributing and playing a major part in his business.

Things didn't last for long. Our first disagreement was my career choice. My goals for my life were to start a beauty empire and my dad wanted me to go to law school. Maybe if I would have just gone with the plans he had for my life, things would have been different between us. Remember I said I had fantasized my whole life and about how my life would be? The industry for me was the beauty industry. I was also willing to do mostly anything my dad wanted me to do so that I could keep him in my life. By this time, I was amazing when it came to makeup. I was also into fashion. My goal was to launch my own line one day. I still haven't done that yet, but I have designed some amazing wedding dresses. If my dad could have just seen what the fashion and beauty industry meant to me then things may have turned out different. But he didn't and because he didn't, it was the beginning of the downfall of our relationship.

Shortly after my dad and I continued to disagree about my career choice he slowly went distant. I almost made myself sick thinking of how I could get us back on the same page. I was hoping that things would get back on track. It didn't. He had met a new woman who was very close to my age and soon our relationship was non-existent again. The arrangement that he had with me to keep all the new business accounts in my name and him paying my bills had started to come to an end. I didn't know it right away, but he was late paying my rent. When I found I was so scared, and this was the first time that I had been on my own. I didn't know the eviction procedure. I thought any day my landlord could just throw me and all my things out into the streets. I was so scared that by this time, I had found a job. I hadn't made enough money yet to pay my bills. I was so hurt and scared. I felt like that girl who had been disappointed by my dad all over again. Just a few months back I was on top of the world. I had finally been welcomed into my dad's life. He was finally accepting me.

I had done everything he needed for him to welcome me into his life. At the time, I was even dieting. I knew he hated my weight, and my plan was to transform right before his eyes. That didn't last long because once my dad stopped paying my rent and I didn't know how long it would take my landlord to throw me out, I was eating more than ever.

Food was what comforted me at any time in my life. Starting as young as I could remember whenever my life was falling apart, I found comfort in food. The more I called my dad and he didn't answer the more I ate and ate until I made myself sick. Finally, one day he answered. I was frantic and he was unbothered. He gave me this lame excuse about work dismissing any of my feelings. All he wanted to do was talk about his new relationship with a girl twice his age and brag about the things he had brought her. I was furious but I held my composure. I needed my dad to stick to the plan or I would be homeless. I had nowhere to go so I tried hard to stay on my dad's good side.

I didn't know the term at the time for what type of person my dad was but now I know my father was a narcissist. After listening to him brag about all the lavish gifts he gave his girlfriend and him scolding me about my life decisions my dad agreed and said that he would pay my rent. He told me it was up to me to remind him each month which was confusing too because I did remind him. I had been constantly calling him. Nothing had changed except the new young girl he had in his life and the fact that I refused to go to college to prepare to be a lawyer like him. As much as I wanted to scream, cry, and tell my dad how he was making me feel, I didn't. I just put my feelings to the side. I didn't realize how much my parents had damaged me until writing this book.

After hanging up with my dad I was confident that he was going to pay my bills like our agreement and our relationship would get back on track. I had resentment towards the new young woman in his life who he was spending all his time and money on. It was obvious she was using him. He looked as if he could be her grandfather. Maybe my dad wasn't as confident as I thought he was. Maybe spending money was his love language. I wonder why he wouldn't just get someone that was closer to his age. I have so many questions. I really only knew my dad on the surface. I didn't really know him. I don't know much about either of my parents' lives, but at least I have the option to ask my mom about her life. I don't have the same option for my dad. Unfortunately, he is no longer here.

After a couple of days, my dad was still not holding his end of the bargain to pay my bills. I thought I would reach out to him again. The phone calls that we were sharing in the beginning of our agreement were now few and far in between. I was once again disappointed by the man I loved the most in the world. He didn't ignore my phone calls this time, instead he just made an excuse about something about him and his new girl. By this time, I was fed up with him. I was tired of his excuses and his lies. I waited a couple of days for him to right his wrongs and stick to our agreement. I was fed up with his stories about how he was chasing around this young woman twice his age and buying her affection. I was over everything. That day I went into survival mode. I was clearly on my own again. I wasn't as scared this time because both my parents had pushed me to the side for so long, I was getting used to it. I was too old for a group home and couldn't go back to the Job Corps I had already graduated from. I damn sure wasn't going into a shelter. I had nowhere to go. It was time I did what I had to do for myself unapologetically.

I went to the bank and took out enough to cover my expenses. I knew my dad was going to probably be mad, but I didn't care. As long as my bills were paid for a few months, I would be fine. It was time I got out there and really hustled, really worked my butt off to get the life that I always wanted. I promised myself I would never again put my life in anybody's hands. It was up to me to create the glamorous life that I wanted and from that day forward I started to use my makeup skills to help me begin to build my dream. My dad didn't realize right away that I had withdrawn money out of his account but when he did, he was pissed, and I didn't care. I wasn't stealing.

The money was in my name, and I could have taken it all. I should have taken it all.

He was spending all his money on women that cared nothing about him anyway. For a few days, I didn't answer his calls. Now he knew how I felt. When I did answer, we got into the worst argument ever. He said some things that hurt me, and I did the same. Things got pretty heated. Somehow, he removed my name from the accounts, and we were done with each other.

Maybe my mom was right about him, but they had both been bad parents in my eyes. That was the last time we were on good terms. I worked my butt off and I would never have to ask my parents for anything again. I thought that maybe he would apologize, or we would agree to disagree but it never happened. We never mended our relationship. When I heard that he had died I was so hurt and angry at the same time. The man that I put on a pedestal all my life left this earth without telling me that he loved me as much as I loved him. Without telling me he was proud of me. I know it sounds selfish, but it's not. I just want the love story I played in my head forever to have a happy ending. I want my daddy to say goodbye and tell me how much he loves me. I want to be affectionate, but it will never happen. We will never get the chance to say goodbye or to have the relationship that I dreamt of all my life. My memories of him will never be loving. It's just something.

Because of the way my father treated me, I dated all the wrong men. I allowed men to walk over me and use me.

I allow them to degrade me because of my weight. His emotional abuse has caused me to be attracted to men who emotionally abuse me over and over again. The same way he made me feel, I now allow men to treat me the same way. So in case there are any men out there reading this story, I have a message for you: You have to teach your daughters how a man is supposed to treat her. Not by telling her. By showing her. You have to lead by example or when she is old enough to date she's going to run into men that use and abuse her. If my dad is looking down on me I know he has a lot of regrets. It must hurt to see his little girl hurt over and over again.

My Journal

September 11, 2018

Do you know what it's like to feel abandoned? When your stepdad makes your mom give you a way to the system when you're 13? Do you know what it feels like to have your whole world turned upside down? Do you know how it feels to be ripped away from life as you know it only to be placed in a facility with 55 other girls? Some were criminals, foster kids and there were even some that suffered from mental health issues. I was so emotional, scared, angry, and hurt all at the same time. I was left there until I was eighteen with little to no visitation from either of my parents. Do you know what that feels like? My mom said she had 3 others to look after, and I was just in too much trouble. She couldn't handle me anymore.

Really, I just didn't fit in. MOM YOU RUINED ME. You could have just taken out the time to see me and try to see what I needed. Maybe I am not good enough to love mom. I mean you told me out of your mouth I would never find a man to love me if I don't lose weight. Well guess what, I don't care anymore! I no longer want a relationship with you. Just go have a drink and watch me reach my next accomplishment as a person.

I wish I knew back then when I first wrote this that my anger and hurt was only holding me back. I never got any real apologies and explanations, every now and then the anger resurfaces. It's usually because she is doing something to trigger me. Her lack of support and love should be something that I'm used to but it is still a hurt I can't seem to control. For a while the hurt has turned into anger. I don't think that we will ever be able to have a healthy relationship. I used to pray to pray for it but now I really don't have an interest. For now, it changes like the weather. My parents really messed me up emotionally.

Dear Mom,

September 15, 2018

Do you miss my mom? I wish that we were closer, but I guess I wished that my entire life. I wish you would support me instead of telling me to just quit. I wish that you would hear my cry for help and just hug me. I wish out of the 2 years of living in Vegas, you would come and see me instead of blaming me for moving away. I wish you wouldn't always put a man in front of your kids and when that same man left you turned to the bottle. I wish you knew how much you hurt me. You broke my heart. I wish you would love me the way that I love you.

I wish that when I tried to talk to you about my feelings you wouldn't put the blame on me. I'm not the mother. That's your job. For some reason, you always thought the role of a mother had an on and off switch. Sometimes I really need you but you're never around. It breaks my heart that I get more support from strangers than you. I inspire millions of girls around the world. Did you know that mom? Did you know that the one thing that made you ashamed of me made me who I am today? All the abuse that you allowed me to endure made me stronger than ever. It has always hurt me that you could be bought. As long as a man has money and is taking care of you, he calls all the shots. You allowed me to be abused, spit on, told I was worthless, fat, and stupid. Just as long as the bills were paid, right mom? When he cheated and left you, I was still there for you. Remember when you let me and my brother sleep on the salon floor for two months when I lost my house in California because my heart was broken, and I was at my lowest point? You told me I couldn't even sleep on your floor. Through all the hurt, I still love you mom. You only get one mom, right? We can't pick our parents, right? We are so different. My heart is so big and pure, while your selfishness has gotten you where you are today. Alone and dealing with another cheating man. Karma?

Sincerely,

Your Estranged Daughter Jamie

My relationship with my mom is simply toxic as hell. She has never loved me the way that I believe that I should be loved. We were ok when it was just us but ever since I could remember she has always put her relationships with men before me. It was like she worshipped the men in her life. They were her superheroes. If things were off with her and the man in her life at the time, her life was totally non-functional. I didn't get it back then. I held so much resentment towards her but working through some of my feelings with this book, I'm able to really try to see things from her side. I admit this process wasn't easy. I can be selfish sometimes which I got from both of my parents. The fact was that I was fending for myself for the majority of my life. I'm facing all my fears and skeletons in this book so I can let some things go in order to heal. I have been bitter for way too long so it's up to me to continue to grow. The resentment I have for my mom is something I have to let go. In order for me to become healthy, I have to start with my mental health. The forefront of depression and anxiety starts with my relationship with my parents. One of my biggest hurdles is forgiving my mom. The resentment I have towards her runs deep.

I'm ready to let it go. It's so hard because just last week, we were arguing via text.

Lately, I have been feeling really hurt that through the years I fought for my life, and she was only here for about a week. They left me to fight for my life on my own. If they were around more and I felt loved, things would have never gotten this bad. In the many years that I've been in Vegas, I can count on my hand how many times my mom has been here to visit me. I was left for dead with people who didn't really know me that were left to take care of me. I showed up when I was the sickest, I've ever been. She literally stayed for less than a week and hasn't been back since. I'm used to being alone. I have done it for so many years. I'm used to my mom not showing up for me, but I almost died.

You know when you enter the hospital, and they ask you who to call in case of an emergency? It should be an easy question, right? It's not for me. Yes, I can put down my mom, but the truth is she has never in real life been my emergency contact for years. Mentally or physically, she has never been there. Do I think she's ashamed of me? Yes. She is only happy when I have a big accomplishment she can brag about. Like being on the news or getting this tv show. I guarantee if my tv show is a hit, I will see my mom more than ever before.

Alcohol and men are her life, and I don't fit in but she spends time with my siblings. Why does this even hurt me so much? I don't know but it's been this way for years. My mom has always treated me differently from my siblings. Remember, she put me in a group home in my early teen years? From there, our relationship was never the same. I used to think it was just my step dad that got in the way of us being close but when he left nothing changed in our relationship. She just found another man and eventually she became consumed with him. It was like a cycle. It was as if she couldn't function if she didn't have a man around. This is one of the biggest things I despise about my mother and yet I inherited some of this toxic behavior. Men didn't give me that security like they did my mom. I was the security. I would financially take care of men to be with me and make excuses for me. I learned that from my mom. She always made excuses for the men in her life no matter what they did.

In my healing process I began to look at things from my mom's point of view which isn't easy because our relationship is still really broken. I have to be honest, she had a rough upbringing. My mom's mother died at an early age and even before her death, my grandfather had removed my mother from the home. That was something I had to acknowledge because if my mom never really had a mother then maybe that's why she didn't know how to be a good mother. My only issue with this is that she has been a good mother to my siblings. I don't know a lot about my mother's upbringing. Maybe if we have this conversation in the future then I could understand her more. I do know her life with her father wasn't easy. Her father would drink a lot and for whatever reason he would beat my mom. When she was in her early teens, he kicked her out of the house and into the street. Sound familiar?

When she met my dad who was a grown man close to 40 and she was a teenage girl. My mom got pregnant with me when she was 17 and what happened after that was a mystery to me. My dad said my mom broke his heart by having a relationship with his best friend. My mom said my dad broke her heart. Maybe if I knew more of the story, I would know how to handle my relationship with my mom better. What I do realize is that she has been through a lot of hurt and maybe her getting pregnant at an early age with me added to the trauma. I still have so many questions. I can't wrap my mind around what a middle aged man was doing with a teenage girl. Sometimes I wonder if my mom's resentment toward me comes from my dad. I never took the time to really hear my mom's story. Maybe that will be a part of our healing process.

Although my mom and my relationship were toxic, I have to give it to her because she was a provider. We never went hungry. I always had nice things and lived in a suburban neighborhood. My mom came from South Central, but she made sure her kids were raised in the valley. We endured a lot of abuse to live this type of lifestyle. Her boyfriend's always had money but weren't always the nicest. I would get beat by my mom's boyfriend. My step father, her husband even went as far as to spit in my face. My mom would put up with cheating and emotional abuse just so our lifestyle could stay the same. I wonder what her thought process was. I wonder how much pain she was in with all she endured. Maybe my mom didn't know how to love me. She was never affectionate. I used to beg her to

spend time with me. I CRAVED
PHYSICAL CONTACT FROM HER.
There were never any hugs, kisses, or
cuddles for me. I guess my mother's love
language for her children was to sacrifice
her happiness so they could have a
different life than she had. Maybe
removing me from the household was a
part of the sacrifices. Removing me still
didn't stop her perfect lifestyle from
collapsing.

My step father's cheating ways
would soon catch up to him and the
perfect world my mom was trying to build
would all come tumbling down. My mom
didn't take it well. I believe this is when
the drinking started. If I could have a
better relationship with my mom I would.
I just really don't know where to start. I
know in order to heal myself, I have to
start by healing us. The pain from my past

causes so many problems in my life. The way I love, my self-esteem, my decision making, being bitter, overeating, anxiety, depression, and the need to be ACCEPTED. For so long I had a void in my life, and I searched for it in other places. I needed affection. I needed to be in love. I need people to see me. I mean really see me. I blame my mom for my family dynamic more than anything. My relationship with my siblings is really non-existent.

My mom had 4 kids. Two girls and two boys. I'm the oldest. She then had 3 children with her ex-husband. Because I was removed from the house so early on, I have always struggled to have a relationship with my siblings. I was closest to my youngest brother. He lived with me a couple times throughout the years. He was always disregarded by my mom as well. So, I connect with him differently than the others. I saw her looking at him the same way she looked at me. Like we weren't good enough. My brother has always had learning disabilities. He didn't learn like most so to mom he was just too much trouble.

Once I noticed how she treated him, I became attached to him. I know how it felt to be in his shoes to crave the love of my mom. To have her embarrassed of your existence. It was as if my youngest brother and I had ruined her perfect picture of what the perfect family she always wanted would look like. It wasn't in her plan to have an obese daughter and a son with learning disabilities. If she would just take the time to spend with us, she would see how much of a big heart we both had.

My little brother was so loving. His personality was everything and I missed him so much. It's been years since I saw him. When I moved to Vegas, he moved back with his dad. As much as I disliked his father for the way he treated me, I'm glad my little brother has someone to take care of him. He was my mom's last child and after the divorce she was ready to party, so he experienced a lot of the same neglect that I did. My step dad was done with her so she was done with my brother being a burden to her. Once I become healthier, my brother will be the first person I want to see. He's the only person I haven't seen at all since I've been here. I saw my other two siblings twice. My little brother isn't capable of traveling on his own and I guess he is too much of a burden for the rest of them to bring him along.

They all came for a few days when I was in the hospital. They had no idea how sick I was, but they still didn't bother to bring my baby brother. He's the only family member I've ever been close to and the only person that has ever loved me unconditionally. I pray every day that I get to spend time with him again. I pray that he is happy and healthy and one day we can be together again.

My other brother is the first son my mom had. He was the oldest after me. He and I didn't have a real good connection. We used to. I pretty much helped raise him. He was my peace when we were younger, but once I was kicked out the house our connection was no longer there. Whatever my mom and step dad told him about me he must have believed because he and I didn't have any type of connection. He was my mother's favorite child and it wasn't like she hid it. It was obvious. He had a lot of my mom's ways. I guess that was the reason they got alone. He was bossy and opinionated. When I got really sick my mom, Jeff, who is my oldest brother, and my sister Jordan came to see me. I was the sickest I had ever been in my life and didn't even know if I would make it. What I remember the most is how I felt being in the presence of my family that I haven't seen in years.

I remember wishing that they had flown into town to see me at my best. Whether it was the opening of the salon or while I was shooting my tv show, I questioned why they had to see me like this? I will never forget the look of disgust my brother gave me when he had to help me roll over and the surprise on their faces when they saw how big I had gotten. Being with your family is when you should feel the most comfortable, but I didn't. As much as I had longed to be with my family and fix our relationship, I found nothing but embarrassment in the room. My brother couldn't hide his disgust and I haven't been able to forget the look on his face.

My relationship with my sister is probably the most disappointing to me. I used to have so much that I wanted to share with her. I was in the fashion and beauty industry and my sister was beautiful and thin like my mother. I wanted to share my knowledge of beauty products and tips with her. I wanted to buy her beautiful things that I wasn't able to wear. She was my baby sister so everything I learned I wanted to teach her. For a while things were great. We had a sisterly bond. She was super protective of me, and I was protective over her. I always felt my mom and I were playing tug of war with her. I wanted to teach her to build a business or find something that she loves and be independent but my mom wanted her to find a husband and security so she would be taken care of. My sister was really shy and quiet, so her personality was a little different than mine and our mother's.

My mom wasn't around much after the divorce, so she missed a lot of the years Jordan needed her most. My sister wasn't bitter like I was. If she was, she would hide it. Eventually, she took my mom's advice and got married. She became a tax accountant and now has a beautiful little girl that I haven't seen since she was a toddler. She won her second marriage following in the footsteps of our mother.

Every issue that my siblings and I have stems from our mother. The messed up part is that she doesn't care. You may not believe this, but I believe it benefits my mom to have us at each other's throats. I think I took some of her toxic traits of divide and conquer when I was trying to hide my real life from the world. I developed a lot of messy traits. I didn't have the skillset, but I could manipulate situations well. so I pulled from my mom's energy. It must have been something I inherited from her without

even knowing because I became very good
at it.

PROM QUEEN

Built to be a queen, an invincible force. She manifested with ease. Magic in every thought. All that she knew is no longer with her imagination. Lifted never to return each negative pattern. The belief of her past has shifted now, using the universe to ignite her power.
She is unstoppable, extraordinary, in every way. A queen of manifestation, all the doubt fell away. The magic intertwined all through my being. Part of reality that goes unseen. She opened up her arms wide and let anyone in. For she knows the power in and out of being. The queen of manifestation bestows her blessing. She bestows her blessings accepting your gift and begins manifesting. May all your dreams come true. She is Queen. She is ME.

Pages in my journal:

I'VE known 3 great loves early on in my life. Each one left me broken...

My first love but also my first domestic abuser:

When you fucked my best friend in my house, in my room while I was sleeping, that broke my heart so bad. You almost made me lifeless. I was betrayed by the closest two people in my life. I was a fool and forgave you. When you put a knife to my neck and tried to kill me and that ... that was my breaking point. It was one of the hardest things I ever had to do but I had to get away from you. Why was my love not enough? I never knew why but loving you taught me how to love myself more. God bless you.

When we were 18 standing on the corner of 11th and Broadway in downtown Los Angeles, you made me laugh and smile. I thought the world of you. Who would have known you would turn out the way you did? I remember struggling to go to work at 5 A.M. Walking to my car by myself while it was still dark outside, while you laid in my bed all cozy. You had nowhere to be because I was your meal ticket. When you put that knife to my neck and threatened to kill me, that was it. It was the breaking point. Walking away from you was one of the hardest things I ever had to do, but I had to get away from you. You were toxic and I already had enough toxic relationships in my life.

Because of this, I never recognized it until it was entirely too late. Why wasn't I enough for you? I would never know. I hope you found someone to love you. God bless you.

My second love:

You always made me laugh and smile. I always thought the world of you. Who would have thought you would turn out to be who you are? I would have never thought you would have been such a user. You quickly changed from the guy who made me laugh all the time to the guy who was draining me. I remember struggling to go to work at 5a. Walking to my car before daylight all by myself while you lay sleeping peacefully. I used to be so mad that I would slam the fucking door because I was so angry that you would just sit around and allow me to not only take care of you, but take care of your 3 year old son as well. All of your responsibility became mine and you didn't even really love me. I don't even think you even liked me, but you liked the stability I offered. I have always been the girl who gave too much to keep the attention of a man. Thinking back, I believe this is where it really started. You didn't hesitate to make me feel like if I wasn't giving you a comfortable lifestyle then you wouldn't be with me. I worked so hard to keep you in my life. It must have been nice to have a woman like me. A woman that loved you so much that they would make anything happen to make you happy. A woman who sacrificed their happiness to make you happy.

I never saw myself as the prize. I am still dealing with that to this day trying to find my worth. I was so young and dumb back then. I lost five years of my twenties that I could never get back. It was five years of training myself to think I wasn't enough. I already had daddy issues, but that relationship gave me even lower self-esteem. I will never get back the time I wasted on you. Love is blind right? Love is so blind. In a blink of an eye, it can all just fade away. Love is complicated. It's a powerful word. Every time I used it, I meant it. I can't say the same for the people I was telling it to. Anyone can say they love you but deep down you know if they're telling the truth or not. I knew that you didn't love me. I knew that I was more of your security blanket.

At the time, which was a hard pill to swallow. I was willing to be ok with it because I was lonely. Being around people who depended on you more than they loved you, can turn you into a different person. The fact that someone could fake loving someone just to use them is so sad to me. I used to write poetry about love all the time making them rhyme. I can't even make up my mind about how to tell you love is blind. You would think I learned from mistakes, but it didn't stop there. It gets worse. This was only the beginning of my lesson. I would keep walking into the same types of relationships.

I bought him anything he wanted or needed without even knowing I was paying for love and all I got was more pain. It was like they singled me out. I never knew that there were men who preyed on fat girls at that time, but I would learn all of that later. They felt as if we had low self-esteem. The sad part is that most of us did. Some of the most successful were the biggest prey. The women who always preached being confident and loving the skin you're in were the targets. I fit right into the category. It was like they saw right through our bull shit and were able to see our fears. They got off on our real insecurities and used us. This happened to me in every relationship I have ever been in. The thing is when I learned about these types of men and what signs to look for nothing changed.

There were times that I would see all the red flags and still continue to pursue a man that I knew only wanted to use me. I know it sounds crazy but after everything I've been through, I didn't want to be alone. I will do anything to not be lonely. This was something that once again stemmed from my childhood. My parents made me feel lonely. I craved for love in my life even if they didn't love me. Then they were you. My ex-fiancé. My greatest love of all but also the man that ruined me. You taught me people will do anything for money if they are desperate enough. You deserve a round of applause for the show you put on.

I never loved a man quite like you. You were my air, my happiness, my everything. It was just an opportunity for you. I always wanted to ask you if any of this was ever real. 2 years of sleeping next to each other building a life together and for what? For it to be fake. My heart still aches from the pain you caused me, and it has been years that have passed but I can't seem to shake the pain. It still hurts every time I think of you like it was just yesterday. Because of you, I was never the same. Sometimes, I regret going through your phone that night because life as I knew it at the time ended that night. I never would have imagined that I would find what I found. How could you cheat on someone who loves you? How can you say you love me but then break my soul? How could you tell my friends and family you couldn't wait to marry me? To find out that you were only in it for a check. Seven women and you were telling us all the same things. My heart still hurts daily. I pray Karma finds you.

Karma is a pain in the light and the rain
Crying without relief, like rain drops off a leaf
From Karma's vengeful raft, lies that ruin my path
Trying not to fall on the way, attempting to go astray

Hold on to my love, but then he flew away

like a dove

He says he loves but yet I cry because

Karma fried our love dry

I'm trying not to cry now. I still don't know

how

This is not very fun. All I can do now is

run

Run from karma, run from my life. I'm

done with all the strife

Stress has taken its toll. Which is leaving a

gaping hole

In what was once my heat, and not even

love can give it a jumpstart

Now it's my time to end, all I have now is a

lonely end

I can say through everything I still believe in love. I pray I find love one day. I'm thankful for my support. Y'all keep me going daily. Every time I get overwhelmed and every time I want to give up, you give me strength. I love and thank you.

For years I have been a prisoner in my own body being confined to a bed. Not able to do small things like drive a car. I had to sell my luxury car because I could no longer fit in it. This is another example of how everything in my life turned to nothing more than a showcase. I have access to beautiful things, but it really meant nothing because most of these things I couldn't even use. I have a closet full of beautiful garments, make up, and designer bags but I could barely get around. If only I could have just paused for a minute, my life would be different. I had intentions to take over the industry. To make women feel good about themselves again no matter how they looked. I was so busy with the mission I forgot about myself. If I was in the right state of mind at the time, I would have practiced what I preached and really took time out to take care of myself instead of trying to cover up everything with a face full of makeup.

By living a life that was just full of lies and cover ups, I lost everything. I almost lost my life. Mentally, I have been reborn, but I still have so much more to go. I was broke and scared and I literally put myself together. Yes, there's time that I want to give up. I'm not going to tell y'all any bullshit anymore. No more f*cking lies. I almost left this earth trying to keep up with all the lies. Although I lost close to 800 pounds and I'm in therapy to learn to walk again, I still get depressed from my living arrangements. Of course, my space is beautiful because that's who I am, but I barely get to enjoy it because I can barely get around. I dream of going on vacation and walking on a beach feeling the sand between my toes. I wish I could do simple things like walk into a movie theater and watch any movie I want to watch. I want to have a girls night out and laugh and dance with my friends. I crave real love. I just want to live a normal life and do normal things but that's my life.

I lay in the bed every day from sunup to sun down in the same routine every day. I can't take care of myself alone. This is not the life I wanted for myself. I wanted to be free and be positive in the skin I was in. While fighting for the world to accept me and respect me for who I was, I stopped respecting myself. I can even understand how I let this happen and how I became confident in this bed. How I let my health decline. It was like somehow with me taking over this movement I manifested the life of my mentor. Be careful what you ask for in life.

The year I moved to Vegas I was mentally drained. I had just lost the love of my life and I should have been seeking some type of help for depression but instead I had my head in the clouds. Just watching how the movement is growing has given me hope. I wanted to be in the mix and that I was going to Vegas to change my life. I never acknowledge that I was too wounded to try to rebuild. I ran away from the problem at the time, but I would turn to the same shit in Vegas. I didn't know it then but that move would ruin my life. I have to take y'all back a bit so you can really understand the story. For you to even know how broken hearted I was and how I wasn't in my right state of mind. I have to tell you about my relationship with my ex-fiancé. I wrote a little about him, but I need y'all to understand who this man was. Who I was at the time. What I was willing to sacrifice to be in the relationship. I was so blinded by love.

Everyone could see he was playing me but me. He had me so in a trance, I couldn't see that he was using me. I get mad every time I think of it because it wasn't like he was that good at hiding his intentions but my relationship with him is really an important part of the story because his heart break is what sent me to Vegas. To understand how broken I was when I went to Vegas you need to know everything that happened to get me to move suddenly. I met my ex-fiancé at my first BBW Convention and we built our relationship via Facebook. You see as the story goes on, you need to know at this time Facebook was my playground. Most of the people I'm going to tell you about I met on Facebook, and we continued our friendship via Facebook. It was still fairly new and a good way to find people that had the same interest as you. What I didn't know is that there were also people on there that used it as a come up.

People have nice pictures and bad intentions. Yes, I had started to go to a few conventions, but I was still very naive. I hadn't met my tribe yet to tell me about the so-called 'chubby chasers'. That meaning could be very broad. It had different meanings. Some men just really like BBW WOMEN. Then you have some that came to these types of events and followed these Facebook Groups to prey on women to see what they could get from them. Their goal was to find girls who were stable with low self-esteem. This was something that happened a lot in my world. Most women will never admit it because they will never admit to having low self-esteem.

The movement is about loving the skin you're in. The truth is there are so many scared and insecure women at these conventions. So many women that seem confident on the outside, but they are dealing with so much depression on the inside. For some of us it's not about our issues with our body. It's more about other people's issues with our body image. Some may have had issues with their families or been teased in school. Some developed a false sense of strength and wanted the world to think they were super confident, but it was a facade. A lot of the time other women couldn't see it, but it was these guys' careers to find these types of women. The higher up the ladder, the more fucked up they are. I didn't realize it until I just let it resonate and actually hear women's real stories and not the fake, fabulous, lives we try to portray.

When I first met my ex-fiancé, he was scandalous and always looking for some type of come up. Calling him KC would be easy for me because he is from Kansas City. He was gorgeous. When he first started reaching out to me, I was hesitant. I knew deep down he had an agenda, but I blocked that out. He was one of the most gorgeous men I had ever seen, and he was giving me the attention I deserved. I didn't care if he had ulterior motives. In a way, I was getting used to guys who used plus size women. In my head it came with the territory of being plus size.

You have to remember not only was I insecure because of my size but I also had daddy issues and abandonment issues because of my mom. I hadn't been in any serious relationships most of my high school years. I was in the group home. My dating experience wasn't the best. I told myself I was satisfied with the attention I got online. Everyone needs some type of intimacy but for me it was easier if I got my emotional charge from a distance. A long distant relationship suited me just fine. I had only been in one real life relationship, and he slept with my best friend while I slept in the same bed, but I was a different person now. At least that's what I told myself.

I was a boss. I owned my own salon. I had a nice residence and a nice luxury car. I had other side hustles and I was comfortable. KC was infatuated with my lifestyle the same way I was infatuated with my dad. From the outside looking in it looked like an Amazon. What he couldn't see from Facebook was my emotional scars. At that time, I wasn't as messed up as I was once, I got to Vegas. I was still very focused and hardworking. I was young and in the beginning stages of wanting to take things to the next level. All he saw was stability. I lived the lifestyle he had wanted. He had always dreamt of moving to California. I had lived there all my life. His dream was to pursue music. I had already started recording. He had stars and his eyes, and I mistook them for hearts.

I thought that he would fit into my life. I would help him pursue all his dreams and he would forever love me for it. I was so naive. I was willing to buy his attention. I was making one of the biggest mistakes in my life and I couldn't be stopped. My friends and even my sister tried to warn me early on, but I was blinded by love. Before I knew it, he was on his way to move to L.A. to spend his life with me. I had everything all set up. The house was comfortable. I had it set up that he would be able to immediately go to the studio to record. My plan was to make him so happy and secure.

What we did not establish before he came was that he would support himself financially. I had been supporting him a lot when he was in Kansas City so he had just assumed that's how things would continue to go. I didn't make it any better by giving him the lavish welcome. I was so mesmerized by how gorgeous he was. I felt like it was unreal that he even gave me a second look although I always looked my best. I still just had a feeling I wasn't really his type. Deep down I knew he was

using me, but I just blocked the feelings
out.

My plan was to create an amazing life for us and he would have no other choice but to fall in love with me. His dark chocolate tattooed skin and Mid-West Swag was refreshing to me. He was so excited to be in California and to pursue his music. I was so in love. I finally felt like I had found my person and we were building a life together. I was working overtime to make sure we had everything we needed but eventually it got overwhelming to be the only breadwinner in the family. His goal was to come to California to make all his dreams come true and I promised him I would help him. I knew that if I started to break my promise, he would start to resent me. I made these promises. I can be extra sometimes, and I can admit that.

As I said before, I was always told that I lived in a fantasy world, so I might have got his hopes up high. I may have even exaggerated the connections I had. I had to do what I had to keep my word. I had to help to turn this gorgeous, small town, young man into a huge star. If I didn't, my relationship may depend on it. In the back of my head, I knew that if I slacked on being the provider in the relationship it may end, so I kept my promise. I worked overtime just so that his Hollywood experience would be everything that I described. I promised him a glamorous lifestyle and that's what I have to give him. He wanted to be a star and I had to do anything in my control to make that happen.

Not only was I paying all of our bills, but I was also paying for his studio time and all the clothes he needed to network and fit in and the Hollywood scene. I pushed him to network and eventually he found his own group of friends. Here's where the trouble would start, and it took me years before I would realize how he had learned to manipulate me. He knew how to get anything he needed from me. I was deeply in love, and I don't think that was the case for him. I knew he had to have love for me because how could someone be with someone for that long without loving them? I mean, how can someone pretend to be in love for that long and sleep with someone every night that they didn't' love? It's so weird to even think of someone being around someone only for financial gain for years.

Everyone else could see it but me. I would argue with my sister about it all the time. She tried to warn me that he was using me. Everyone around me tried to warn me but my daddy issue affected the way that I loved men. I have this thing about me, something else that I'm working on: I put up with a lot of shit from the men that I'm dating. I allow them to treat me like shit. I get mad at my mom for allowing men to treat her badly, but I have the same traits. I don't put up with anything from former friends who have done me wrong. I will cut them off in a minute, but I allow men to do worse and I stay in it for years. This is one of my biggest flaws.

My ex-fiancé had started to show me signs that he didn't value our relationship, but they say love is blind. I didn't want to see the signs. I would rather just distance myself from the people who were telling me. I was afraid if I even addressed the issue he would leave. By this time, he had met a lot of people. He had started to build his friend group and I wasn't included in it. It was like he had separate lives; he had a life with me and a Hollywood lifestyle. It felt a lot like the relationship I had with my dad. I felt like his world wasn't ready for a fat girl. I felt like he wanted to keep me a secret from his friend group.

Instead of questioning him, I started to question myself. Our distance wasn't his fault, it was my fault. I started to second guess my efforts to give him the lifestyle that I promised I was going to provide when he came to California. Maybe my connection was no longer good enough. The more insecure I got the more disrespectful he got. I worked my ass trying to provide a lifestyle for him I really couldn't afford. I love him and I wasn't going to let this city of shiny things take the love of my life away like it took my dad away from me. It's so weird thinking back how that situation was so similar. How I was fighting for the affection of a man who had become blinded from the Sunny California and flashy Hollywood. This felt so familiar to me, and I was getting weary. I was desperate trying to keep him happy and I was exhausted from carrying us financially. I was tired of him taking my car every day to go God-knows-where. I was tired of the lack of affection, and I couldn't take it anymore.

Although it took him a while because he had come so consumed with his new lifestyle, he realized I was tired. It affected him that I was now taking my car to work and not letting him drop me off. He started to see that I didn't care when he had an attitude when I used to do anything to make him happy. Something must have clicked in his head that I was close to ending things because I was fighting with myself every day to get out of the relationship. I was tired. I didn't know then, but I know it now. He had to do what he had to do to keep me around. He had got bitten by the Hollywood bug. It was no way he was going back to being a small town boy who was just sitting back thinking about making it one day. Even if that meant being with someone he didn't love.

Just like that his behavior changed. We had a conversation about fixing our relationship and he went from night to day just like that. He became extra affectionate. He found a part time job. He didn't keep it long but now he had a reason to take my car again. He started to spend a little more time with me. He started to get back focused on the music. He did what he had to do to seal the deal. He brought a non-expensive ring and asked me to marry him. I wasn't worried about how cheap the ring was. I could update it myself. I was more excited that he had finally shown that he loved me. He was willing to fight for our relationship when he almost lost me. He told my whole family how much he loved me and wanted to marry me. He had everyone willing to give him the benefit of the doubt. I felt vindicated. Everyone who had so much to say how bad he treated me had to eat their words. He had proven himself. He loved me. He appreciated everything I did for him. He wanted to spend the rest of his life with me, and I was back on cloud nine. My head was back in the clouds. I felt so lucky.

What had I done to deserve such a handsome, sexy, talented man? I didn't realize at the time that I was the prize. He should have been thanking God for me. I felt extra confident to have him love me so much he wanted to marry me. I wanted to give everything I promised to him and more. It was time to really level up. I wanted to make him happy, so I did. I started working more to make sure we had more money. I upgraded our car and I started meeting more people in the music and entertainment industry. I made sure he had more studio time. Our living space was fabulous. I made sure he looked good and ate well. I didn't care about the extra work at this time. He was showing me more affection and he seemed to be focused. He wanted to marry me.

I was going to do everything in my power to stay good. The thing was, I didn't have the power he did, and he was making a fool out of me while I did everything in my power to build a life together. Good times didn't last for long. He just got better at playing the game. Soon it all came tumbling down and I was completely blindsided because by this time he mastered playing me and making me think he really wanted to spend his life with me.

The thing was he was such a narcissist and was so comfortable being taken care of, that he would have married me for security. The only thing he would leave me for is if he found a person or a situation that was better.

The only thing I can say is God works in mysterious ways. He started to get so comfortable that he became sloppy again. I didn't notice it because I was still planning my new life and a wedding. Once again, I was in a fantasy world. I was focused on what our future looked like and I completely started to ignore the red signs of the present. My sister was the first person to come to me. This time around, no one wanted to be bothered with trying to warn me. I was completely under his spell, and it wasn't open for discussion. I lost some good friends because of my bad relationships with me. This is something that I still go through with men. It's a big flaw of mine.

Letters in my journal

I promise myself
To be so strong that nothing can
Can disturb my peace of mind
To talk health happiness and prosperity
To every person I meet
To make all my friends feel
That there is something in them
To look at the sunny side of everything
And make your optimism come true
To think only the best and work for the
best
And expect only the best, and to expect
only the best
To be just as enthusiastic and the success
of others

As you are about your own
To forget the mistakes of the past
And press on to the greater achievements
of the future
To wear a cheerful countenance at all
times
And give a living creature you meet a
smile
To give so much time to the improvement
of yourself
That you have no time to criticize others
To be to large for worry, to be noble for
anger, and to be strong for fear
And to happy to permit the presence of
trouble
To think well of yourself and to proclaim
this fact to the world
I promise me

I DREAM OF BEING HAPPY

I have dreams of going on vacation to an exotic place surrounded by good people who I love. People who want to be around not because of what I can do for them but people who want to be around me because they actually enjoy my company. I dream of being happy. Laughing not fake laughing. I mean really laughing because I'm happy. I don't even know what being happy really feels like. For so long I kept a fake smile on my face to hide the pain. I dream of replacing the fake smile with a real smile. I dream of real success not fake success. Most people may think I'm successful but that is not true. I have never made a profit from the salon. Yes, I took many risks to live my dream, but I never had much success from the salon financially. I work from home just to keep the doors open. Just to please the world. At this point I don't need to be rich, that was an old dream. Now I just want to be happy, comfortable, and become healthy. I dream of actually being healthy. I dream of being a normal weight. My weight has been controlling the way I live for years and I'm tired.

I have all these dreams almost every night of this wonderful life I want to live. I have been able to manifest so many things in my life. I manifested moving to Vegas and the opening of the salon. I manifested making my mark on the plus size community and all the magazine covers and interviews. I even manifested reality shows and all these accomplishments. I somehow haven't been able to manifest good health and happiness. I dream every night of things that may seem simple to most people but seem impossible to me. When I wake up from the amazing dreams of health, love, and happiness, I wake up in the same nightmare. Many nights when I go to sleep I dream of running on the beach being happily surrounded by love. I wake up confined to a bed fighting to lose weight. Learning to walk again.

My house isn't filled with love like in my dreams. I have two nurses that come to help take care of me. One in the morning and one at night. A physical therapist that comes a few times a week They treat me well but there's no love in my house. On the good side, I was able to manifest material things and one day the things that really matter will start to happen. I've been putting in the work. I'm losing weight and doing what the physical therapist asks of me. Although I feel like my dreams of being happy seem so far away, maybe they are closer than I imagine. Maybe my happily ever after is closer than I feel it is. Maybe it starts with me healing not just my physical health but my mental health.

For as long as I can remember, I have been suffering from depression and anxiety. My brand has always been about me being happy being in the skin I'm in. I have been in the public eye for years talking about how confident I am. I told so many lies about how I loved myself. How all plus size women should love themselves but the truth is that wasn't my truth. I have never been that confident or happy with the skin I was in. I was good at dressing up real pretty and putting on a show for the world. On the internet, I had thousands of fans cheer me on and tell me how they wish they could be as confident as I was but I'm sorry to tell you about this but dolls but I'm not confident. I broke and hurt my dolls.

I suffer everyday with depression, and I want to heal. In order for me to heal I have to be transparent. It's really hard for me but I just can't pretend anymore. I'm tired of dreaming about happiness and sometimes I cry myself to sleep. I'm tired of pretending that my presence can command a room when I have anxiety every time, I step out my door. I dream of one day having the confidence I pretend to have. This season of my life, I'm really trying to heal. I'm no longer telling myself a bunch of lies and I'm no longer lying to my audience. I no longer have to keep up with covering up. It was almost as hard as going through it. It's easier for me when I just tell the truth. I've been lying for so long I almost feel naked with everyone knowing my real story and knowing how the community I fought so hard for made me feel like I had to lie to them to fit in. I'm not going to say that it is something I still don't want to hide because it is.

I don't want the world judging my relationship. I know everyone will have questions about where my so-called boyfriend was when I was going through everything I was going through. It annoyed me that my friend pointed out he only comes around when things are good in my life. I'm not stupid and I know most of these things are true, but these are things I'm not ready to talk about in detail yet, because I'm still going through them. I'm still battling these demons. What I am not going to do is allow anyone to ever hold my story over my head again. That is something that I will never let happen again. I will no longer be a prisoner to my lies.

That doesn't mean that my life is going to be an open book either. It just means it's no longer going to be a fairytale. I'm not trying to be perfect for people who aren't perfect themselves. I'm excited by my new chapter. I can't sit here and lie and say it has been a smooth transition. I promised y'all I was going to stop lying to y'all. Everyone wasn't happy with the new me. They weren't happy that I was telling the truth about the BBW community. They weren't happy I was losing weight or was promoting weight loss products. I had a lot of people who unfollowed me. I had women who were cheering me on a year ago who now hate me. They sent me disrespectful dms and wrote disrespectful comments on my posts.

I have to admit that at first it hurt. I fought with myself. I felt sorry for myself. I did the same thing to the people who had encouraged me to walk in my truth. I blamed everyone I could for the backlash as was getting from the community I had built but I shouldn't have been surprised. They were doing just what the plus size community did. They had proven my point and became mean girls. After I got over feeling sorry for myself and watching my followers decline, I got angry. It was like something just clicked. I remember my mentor and how I wanted to be so much like her. I remember how she died and how similar our fate almost was. She is no longer here but I made it through.

I started thanking God for bringing me through and I started standing up for myself. I now realize something: The people that once was a part of my journey will start to change and I was able to make peace with it. I am not going to continue to be unhealthy to be a part of a group. As I change, my tribe will change. My friends will change and maybe really soon my environment will change. I could have died but I didn't. I'm still here for a reason and now my prayer for once in my life is to be able to live. I still have a long journey and I still have a lot of weight to lose but everyday I'm not only working on my physical health I'm working on my mental health as well. My mental health is what got me here in the first place. I'm thankful for the future and my dreams are getting more vivid.

My Mentor

I first met my mentor at a body positive convention in Las Vegas. I was so excited to be there, I had to pinch myself. It was everything I thought it would be. It was a cool experience following the tribe on social media but to be there in the mix of everything was surreal. There were beautiful plus size women everywhere. I was so happy to be included and had finally found my tribe. I had been to a few BBW conventions but something about this one was different. I felt more at ease. I had a rough couple of months, and I didn't want to think about it. I just wanted to have fun. It was time to live my life for myself. I had been living it for other people for a long time. I wanted a new life. I was tired of the heartbreaks. It was time to put love on the back burner. I couldn't take any more heart breaks. It was time to live my best life.

I had a lot of dreams I needed to pursue. I was doing well in life, but it was time to really turn things up a notch. I didn't have a plan at the time, but I felt by being there, I had taken the right steps. The people were so glamorous. I was right where I was supposed to be, and I looked the part. I had hand made my outfit and everything about it was on point. My makeup was flawless, and my accessories were over the top. My purse and shades were designer. I had an agenda. I was going to take the movement by storm and get my seat at the table to be in the room with the people in the industry. I had a lot to offer. My salon had already made a name for itself in California, and I had been in the media. I had a huge up and coming influencer who had written about me in their book. I was at the top of my game.

I have to admit, I was intimidated by some of the girls. They were not as friendly as I thought they would be. It was the first time I got to see the mean girl side of the industry. Yes, although the movement has the word positivity in it, there are a lot of negative people in it. I didn't get it before but since I've been through so much throughout the years, I get it now. We were a bunch of beautiful women who were told we were not good enough by people because of our sizes. For some women, it made them powerful. Some became bitter. Some had both traits and I believe it can be a dangerous personality. I know because eventually I became that bitter, popular girl. It was hard to not be in that type of environment even after everything I had already been through. Remember at the time I was dealing with a freshly broken heart? I didn't heal. I thought about coming to the conventions meeting new people. Everyone had a story and some of the girls were happy to be there, but they were on guard. They wanted to be the "IT" girls at the conventions. The guys who attended the events did not help either. Some of them were there because they really liked plus size women, and they were looking for a connection. Then you had the one that was just there to suck the energy out of the room. To find women they can use and abuse. I was finally able to see the situation I had just got out of was normal in our community.

There were men out there that were targeting plus size women, and it wasn't a secret. It was something that the women in the community had learned to deal with. It sounds horrible when I say this out loud because it was what it was. At that time, I had just been through the biggest heartbreak of my life. I found that the man that I was going to marry was just using me for financial gain and from speaking with some of the women at the convention, I found out that this was a common thing. I had my mind set that this would never again be a part of what I was going through in life. I didn't have the time for that type of energy. I had my mind made up after what I had just endured with my ex.

Life was going to be full. No drama. I was going to live the type of life I had always wanted to live. That's when I began spending time with Juanita. I met her at the conventions. I could see from day one, she was the girl that everyone adored. She was someone that I needed to know. People gathered around her like she was a celebrity. She had this look about her that said BOSS. She was just as flashy as I was. She greeted everyone. She had that IT factor. Although she was much older than most of the girls there, everyone seemed to know her name. I knew she was somebody that I wanted to meet, and I was shocked when she introduced herself to me. From that day we became fast friends.

Juanita was everything that I wanted to be. She had the plus size community on lock. She had a club for all plus sizes she did once a month. The first time I stepped foot in one of her parties I felt like I belonged. There were beautiful plus size women and handsome guys everywhere. I have never had that much fun in my life. Juanita sat in her section looking like the queen that she was, and she allowed me to be amongst her and her crew. She took me under her wing. We shared similar stories.

We both had our hearts broken, we both were passionate about the plus side community, and we both were flashy. She was one of my biggest supporters when it came to taking the body positive salon to the next level. She was a savvy business woman. From the outside looking in Juanita, had the life that all of us plus size girls dreamed of but deep down like all of us, she was fighting her own demons. On the outside, it looked like she had everything someone like me could have.

For the next few years, my mentor and I became amazing friends. I thought I wanted her life. She had accomplished everything I thought that I ever wanted. She was the H.B.I.C in the plus size industry and she always told me she was training me because soon she would be retiring. I wanted so badly to be like her. I was going to take the plus industry by storm just like she did. I was going to build a team just like her and that team was going to help me take over the industry with her knowledge and my ideas. I would be at the top in no time. I was obsessed with her lifestyle and what she had accomplished. You know the saying: be careful what you ask for? Well, it was real.

Months later my mentor went from running the city and handing down the plus size parties and her connections to me. In my head I thought it was because she had made enough money to retire. That was far from the truth. The truth was her health was declining and she could no longer get around anymore. By the time I was all settled in, she was completely bed bound. That amazing team I thought she had was long gone and left her for dead after most of them had stolen everything they could get. Every time I spoke to her, she was telling me how people were stealing from her. My worst regret was I never took the time to be the friend to her she was to me. I was always too busy. Also, at this time, I was working hard on trying to keep my new salon afloat and taking care of the monthly parties I had taken over for her. Within a few months she died, and I never got a chance to say goodbye.

A few years later I found myself going through the same exact things that my mentor was going through. I had come to Vegas for her to hand me her crown and now our fates were intertwined. I was now bed bound. I wasn't able to get around and the people around me were robbing me dry. It reminded me of Marilyn Monroe and Anna Nicole. Did I look up to this woman so much that I had inherited her fate? Well, it may be going in that direction but I want to live. If I had spoken to my mentor before she died, I may have prevented some of the things I went through. I learned 3 big lessons. Be careful what you ask for. The plus size community can chew you up, spit you out, and move on like nothing ever happened. R.I.P to my beautiful mentor I will never forget you.

Roommates From Hell

I was never planning on having a roommate. I quickly realized that I needed a roommate. I was living in my dream house. I had way more space than I ever had in California for half the rent I was paying. What I didn't know is that my dream salon wasn't going to take off like I thought it would. I thought that all the press was going to turn the business into a hit. I was expecting for the money and success to come rolling in, but when a new month came rolling around, I had to pay my bills out of pocket. I hadn't even made enough to cover my expenses. I didn't know it at the time but that would become my life. Robbing Peter to pay Paul. Once again, to this day my salon has never made a profit. I know you're probably surprised. You're probably thinking I must have been insane to continue to do something that was causing me that many problems, but you have to understand: It was my dream. I couldn't give up on something I loved so much. I had to do what I needed to do to make things work.

Now let me just remind you of the state of mind that I was in. I had just broken up with my fiancé and in less than a year, I had packed all my things up and moved to a new city. No family or friends other than my mentor Juanita, who was busy running her own business and had started to become sick due to weight issues. As I told yall, I was talking to a guy who had abandoned me the first week I got there. So, if I was going to make this dream work, I was going to have to do two things: get a roommate and continue to work my second job from home. I quickly realized that I had to do both. I had a few girls stay a few weeks, but my first real roommate was the best roommate ever.

In Las Vegas there is a big adult entertainment industry for plus size women and that is what she did for a living. She brought a lot of clients to my business. It was a dream and what she did for a living wasn't an issue to me. She was never late on the rent. She was always recommending our salon to people, and she was well known. I admired how she handled herself. She was glamorous and beautiful. We never argued or disagreed. A lot of the time, she wasn't there. She traveled a lot. She loved to travel and find new opportunities. She was just as ambitious if not more than I was. It felt good to finally be around a go getter. Although I felt a lot of pressure, it was people moving to Vegas just to be a part of Babydoll Beauty Couture. I know a lot of them wouldn't believe it now because of how things ended but I took it very seriously that people had relocated to be a part of the brand that I was building. I thought it would be more successful and a good financial move for us all.

I didn't understand at the time that the same community I was fighting for wasn't fighting or supporting me. I also didn't understand that a lot of people were confused about the message of the salon. Some people refused to come because they thought it was only a plus size salon. The goal was to make everyone feel included, but I alienated people and that wasn't my intention. The plus size community can be very intimidating. Some of the people I hired to put the word out and made it what they wanted to be. I wasn't paying much attention, I was just trying to keep the doors open. Having a roommate like my first roommate kept me motivated when I really wanted to break down in tears.

Although the shop wasn't really making money yet, I was still living my dream life. I had good work from home and a beautiful home with a great roommate who always paid on time. Juanita had molded me and trained me to take over the club night once a month. I was in the studio doing music again and was in the stages of creating a new cosmetic line. What I didn't know was that things wouldn't stay good. I would eventually lose my perfect roommate. It was like someone removing a security blanket and it couldn't be at a worse time.

She was dating this older man who started out as a sugar daddy and ended up exclusive. He was ready for her to move in and I was going to have to lose my perfect roommate. I was pissed at the time. I know I should have been happier for her, but I couldn't. I already had abandonment issues. At this time, I felt like I was being abandoned left and right. The stylist was quitting because the salon wasn't making any money. I wasn't going in there much because I was working overtime from home just to keep the doors open. I felt the plus size community had abandoned me because they weren't supporting me like I thought they would. I would support the convention and plus size and body positive community so much. I could barely get them to come through my doors. I didn't know it at the time, but I quickly learned the salon was in one of the worst parts of town. It was like everything was hitting me all at once. The perfect life that I wanted was no longer perfect.

My mentor wasn't really a mentor anymore. Her health had gone from bad to worse and the pain pill addiction had started. When I did speak with her, I didn't understand what she was talking about because she was medicated. Things were just bad for me and when my roommate said she was leaving, I felt more alone. I thought about going home because everything was falling apart. We had been living with each other for almost two years and she must have felt bad because a couple of weeks before she left, she told me she had another roommate for me. I didn't believe it at the time, but she would be the roommate from hell.

Roommate number two was a wolf in sheep's clothing. I would have never expected how my life would be once she entered it. She was recommended by roommate number one who had been the perfect roommate, so I was expecting her to be similar. Roommate number 1 had vouched for this woman. She said she was one of her closest friends. I had no reason not to trust what roommate number 1 told me. If she said roommate number 2 was a perfect roommate, then I believed her.

When I first met roommate number 2 I was nervous. I had enough problems in my life at the time so if things didn't work out, I didn't know what I would do. I didn't want to lose my beautiful home because it was everything I dreamed of. The part of the house that I was renting was its own separate part of the home. The realtor called it a mother-in-law suite. It had its own kitchen, bathroom, and entrance. It was like having your own apartment. I had a pool and a nice size yard. I was lucky to have found such a beautiful home and I didn't want to lose it. If there were any red flags in the beginning, I would completely block them out. Never make an important decision when your back is against the wall. Just maybe if I was in a different situation at the time, I would have been able to really pay close attention to roommate number 2 at our first meeting. Maybe if roommate number 1 would have given me a notice, I would have had a chance to interview multiple roommates. I have to admit I had a funny feeling about roommate number 2 but I pushed it to the side. What other choice did I have?

When I first met her, she was lovely and friendly. She said she also traveled a lot and wouldn't be here that much. She also was in the adult industry, and she had big dreams just like I did. The difference was I had a plan and she really didn't. All she just kept saying was in the next couple of years. What I didn't know at that time was that she would do just about anything to make it happen. With roommate number 2, it was a totally different vibe as roommate number 1. She wanted to interact more. It took some getting used to because I was used to how things were but what I hadn't admitted to myself was I was lonely. I didn't really plan it until I had someone who wanted to communicate and do things together. We ate together and talked. We even did each other's make-up and watched movies. Her personality was big and fun. She told me early on that she had 3 kids that her ex had custody of, and they came over on the weekends. They came over the first weekend and we had so much fun. I felt like I now had family in

Vegas, and I was able to handle a lot of my problems differently.

I have to admit, roommate number 2 and her girls were a breath of fresh air at first. I wasn't just always working. I was interacting with people, and I wasn't alone anymore. By this time, I wasn't going to the salon at all. I had someone running it and I didn't know it at the time, but everyone at the salon was over me and my dream. They weren't making money. I wasn't coming in that much. I had let myself completely go from all the stress. All I was doing was eating, worrying, and working. It felt good to have a roommate to confide in. I was overjoyed that she wanted to help me. I had no idea at the time, but what she wanted to do was take over my life. She wanted to act like she cared about me and was in my corner just so she could take my place. I know it's weird right? Well, it gets weirder.

The next weekend the girls came to visit, and they never left when the weekend was over. She never even gave me an explanation why they stayed. It was like they moved in. What I didn't know then that I know now, is that they weren't living with their dad. That was just one of her lies and part of her plan. had messed up by telling roommate number 2 my business. I fell for her helpful and overly friendly act. I had no idea I was dealing with someone evil. Someone who would do anything she had to do to get what she wanted. I had told her the business was failing. I told her I was in Vegas on my own with no family. I told her most of the people who were helping me build it were over it because of the lack of cash. I told her I needed to find someone who could help me turn the business around. She told me she wanted to help, and she had a lot of ideas how she could help. Where I had gone wrong was instead of hiring a manager to run the business while I worked, I had my receptionist doing everything. I had just signed with a production company to do a new reality show. I couldn't let the salon go under because if I did the business would no longer exist.

I explained to roommate number 2 that if I could just keep the doors open to tape the show, then it would save the whole brand. She was impressed by what I had built so far and with what I was doing. She promised that she could help me take things to the next level. The old receptionist lasted less than a week after I hired roommate number 2. She had a plan to get rid of the people who were in her way. I had already been played by roommate number 2 so many times in the few months that she was there, and I was so blind. Well, not completely to be honest.

She had started to make me dependent on her. We were moving as a family and the kids were not living their full time. Roommate 2 would cook us meals when she wasn't at our shop. She was helping me promote my cosmetic brand to women in the adult entertainment industry. She was still going away to the adult entertainment conventions and events, so she wasn't in my salon all the time. She was only there when she didn't have a gig. Guess who was left to watch the kids when she was at these conventions? You guessed it right. Me. She would convince me that these conventions would get me more business. I have to admit, I started to get more customers that were from the plus size adult entertainment world. Things were slightly picking up but we had plans to make things really pick up. She had a lot of amazing ideas so I had no reason not to believe her, but things went from good to worse really fast.

Out of nowhere I had become a full time babysitter. I didn't have much time to myself. I worked from home a couple of hours a day to make sure all the bills were being paid but I wasn't able to work as much as I would have liked because I was responsible for three kids. Now roommate number 2 was working at the salon full time, and I was paying her weekly. She was shooting adult entertainment and making appearances on the weekend and started to be late on the rent. She went from being late to barely paying at all. This was the second red flag for me, but this one had more entitlement behind. I should have talked to her at this time. She had changed fast, and Roommate 2 was out all working in her industry but always had an excuse as to why she didn't pay her rent.

She had started to make me feel that I should be happy to have her around and on top of everything she wasn't treating people at the shop well. She was supposed to come in and make things run smoother but instead she came in and caused more trouble. Everyone quit! Now things had gone from bad to worse and it was almost time for me to start shooting my show. On top of everything that was going on, I had a party coming up and had a special guest performer. It was time to level up. I had to hire a new team. I gave roommate number 2 a chance to make it happen and she had done well for a few months. When she got comfortable, she just caused more trouble than ever before. Although there were so many red flags, I just had to stay focused.

I needed to hire a manager to start helping me out with getting other projects, with my music, and cosmetic line. It was time to build a team to help me build and stop me from losing everything I worked so hard for. I knew just the person: Syreeta. She reached out to me a couple of years back. She was doing a tour for one of her clients that was on the tv show Love and Hip Hop at the time. The event went really well, and it was almost a year later but we kept in touch. I would call her for business questions already, so I thought this was the perfect time to bring her in as my manager. My plan was for her, myself, and roommate number 2 to save the brand but it was the beginning of a disaster.

Immediately, my new manager got to work. The thing was, I was trying to hide so much of what was really going on and I wasn't honest with her when I hired her. Everything started out as a lie. Covering up the truth had been a habit that I was developing. I liked to hide how my life was really spiraling. I wasn't honest about how bad the business was really doing. I wasn't honest about being in the beginning stages of being bed bound. At this time, I was able to get around some, but I was getting closer to being bed bound. That was something that I had hidden from everyone, so I didn't volunteer the information with her when I asked her to manage me.

I wasn't thinking straight. How can I hire someone to help me get my life together but not be honest with her about what was really going on? I didn't tell her I was having some speculation about roommate number 2 at all. She loved me and she knew a lot of my secrets. I couldn't risk her telling my new manager about everything that was really going on and have her drop me. I saw how hard she had worked for some of her clients. I thought I could build a team with her and roommate number 2. The second day on the job, I needed her to help me with a crisis. All the staff had quit. Roommate 2 said she was going to help me hire a new staff member, but it had been two weeks and she hadn't said anything else about it. I didn't know it at the time, but she was one of the reasons everyone was leaving.

Let me make this clear because I believe somewhere my message was lost from letting people come along and tell my brand story: My salon is not for just plus size women. My salon is all inclusive. It's a place where all people can feel comfortable no matter their size, race, or creed. Somewhere along the way I let people push this narrative. It was us, never them. They made it like I only wanted to have people from the plus size community come to my salon. That is not what I was trying to do. If it came off that way, I'm sorry. The goal was to make sure I accommodated plus size women by making sure the chairs can hold their weight. had custom chairs made that could hold up close to four hundred pounds.

Roommate number 2 was one of those gatekeepers I put in my salon that made people who were in the plus size community feel uncomfortable. Although I can't just put the blame on her. I have to blame myself. She wasn't the first person who I let come in and push that narrative. Maybe I wasn't explaining myself well enough. Of course, everyone knew why I started the salon but by letting people make it seem like the salon was only for plus size women was like we were doing the same things that were done to us. I was so busy trying to keep the door open. I let my message be spread from different people other than myself. The plus size community can be kind of brutal. A lot of hurt women that have been bullied in the past became bullies. Roommate number 2 was definitely that. I didn't see it at the time because she wore 2 faces proudly. Me telling the stylist one thing when they were hired and her telling them another once they got there was a big mistake.

We weren't able to keep a stylist. They would work there for a week and then they would be gone. Things had begun to spiral out of control. At the time, I thought I could trust roommate number

2. I should have seen right through her. She told me one thing that I still believe to this day that was true. She wanted to be a star. I believe that her goal was to build off of my brand. She saw me as being sickly and she wanted to fill my shoes. The thing was if she was truthful about wanting to build her brand, I would have helped her. She just really wanted to take my brand over. She was so confused. One minute she wanted to be an influencer and one minute she didn't want to be an influencer. The first time I told her no was the beginning of her showing her true colors. I just wasn't prepared for how dark things were about to get and how many lies were being told.

How Did I Become A Hostage?

Have you ever been afraid for your life? I mean really afraid for your life? I have. Not only was I afraid that I would die in my sleep because of my weight, but now I was afraid for a different reason. I was afraid because I was a prisoner in my own home. An unwanted guest that I didn't even know was living in my house for months without my knowledge. The fallout that I had with roommate number 2 revealed a lot of things. I was so clueless, and I didn't know what was happening. You know the saying by having a fallout with someone you may really get to know how they feel about you? In my case, I found out more than I could ever imagine. I found out I was being deceived by the person that I thought I knew. I didn't know who roommate number 2 really was. She had turned into a horrible person.

The arguments had gotten so bad and by this time she was no longer an asset. She became a liability. She was no longer working at the salon. I had started to see things about her I had to address. My manager was over it by then. I had hid so much from her and she couldn't help me. I had told so many lies that our relationship was done. She had a bad feeling about roommate number 2 and I should have listened. Deep down, I had a gut feeling also but roommate number 2 knew too much about me. Things that I was hiding from my tribe. I was hiding from everybody.

Now that I think back, it would have been easier to just tell my real story. It would have been easier to tell my tribe that my life was falling apart. She wasn't paying rent. She was in the adult entertainment industry full time. She had made some connections and was now leeching off someone else. She left the city to do this plus size adult entertainment tour. She left without even telling me, but I would have been ok with that because at the time I was over her. She had started to be more disrespectful than ever. I was ok with her being gone, but she left her kids. I know it even sounds crazy repeating it. This lady left her kids and refused to come back. I was so confused.

Every time I tried to call her she would hang up in my ear. Although I had loved the little girls, I wasn't in any position to take care of them. I couldn't even get out of bed. I was sick and hadn't even been to a doctor at that point. I couldn't take care of any children. I couldn't even take care of myself. I was dying because I was sicker than I could ever imagine. I begged her to come and get her daughters. She left them with no money or food. That wasn't anything new. I had been helping take care of them before they got here. They were so sweet and helpful. I paid them an allowance to help me out around the house.

By this time, my mobility was getting worse and worse. I remember calling her only when I was fed up. It was the first of the month, she had to pay rent and she didn't. She had been spreading all types of rumors about me. All the stylists had left the shop because I hadn't been completely honest with them. My manager had quit because I didn't tell her the truth. Not only did I not tell the truth, but I allowed roommate number 2 to tell my story without a response. She told my story and added more lies. This was the first time all my staff had quit but this was also the first time I didn't have anyone to help me. My problems were piling up. I wasn't carrying just my burdens, I was carrying roommate number 2 and her burdens as well.

I sent her a text letting her know that she needed to come and get her kids. She texted me back that she wasn't coming back. It was a problem now. I couldn't believe it. This woman wasn't a family member. She wasn't someone I knew for years but yet she left me with her kids and refused to come back. She even refused to pay her half of the rent to ensure they would have a roof over their head. I was shocked. I didn't know what to do. I had no one to call. I had pushed everyone away trying to hide my secrets but now everything was out. The world knew I was too fat to get out of bed. At this time, I could still walk but barely. They knew I was broke and my salon would eventually have to close. She exposed some things that were true but because I didn't respond, she told a lot of lies.

Looking back, I realize I was better off telling my own story because she made me look bad. Everyone was talking about me but this time not in a good way. The crazy thing was she was out there trying to tear down my business, but her daughters were still at my house, and I hadn't seen her in almost two weeks. Well, I was over it! I felt betrayed and I wasn't going to let this lady continue to try to ruin me. I woke up one morning with a little more strength. I felt like everyone was turned against me because of her lies. I texted her to come and get her kids again. She texted back that she wasn't coming back, and she had a few other disrespectful comments to say about me paying the kids to help me tidy up. She called everyone she knew spreading more lies about me forcing her kids to clean up after me. I could barely move around but I couldn't force anyone to do anything. She was lying.

What she wasn't telling people was that I was taking care of her kids and I was paying them an allowance in her absence. I was paying allowance for anything else they needed. I had my own problems. My business was failing, and I was working from home doing 10 hr. shifts to try and save it. Since she came into my life, things have gone from bad to worse. This was just the beginning. I couldn't make this up if I tried. I sent her the last text that if she didn't come pick up her kids, I would have to call someone. I was completely over her. She was trying to destroy me and my business. Her oldest daughter came knocking on my bedroom door just as I was looking up who to call. She said her dad was here and he wanted to speak with me.

At first, I was relieved. Remember in the beginning she told me the kids were supposed to live with their dad? Maybe he finally was going to pick them up. Then I could go back to my life and figure out how to pick up the pieces. Maybe I could reach back out to my former manager and former employees to let them know what was going on and apologize for my part. I wasn't sure how I could even get started fixing all the mess around me, but I knew I needed roommate number 2 out of my life. I didn't realize that roommate number 2's baby father wasn't coming to make things right with me. He came into my room and really dropped a bombshell on me that I wasn't expecting.

He wasn't here to pick up the kids! He said he had been living in my guest house for months and paying roommate number 2. Not only had he been staying in my house, he had been receiving mail so that made him a resident. He said it with confidence. I was devastated. I was played as a fool right in my own house. The only way I could get this man out of my house was to take him to court. How did this happen? How did I let these people fool me like this? I was so confused and hurt. I had no control over my life, and I didn't know what to do, I couldn't call my family. They haven't even checked on me in months. I couldn't call my manager because she had quit and no longer believed anything I said. None of my staff was talking to me. They played this well: Divide and Conquer.

I was so scared. His voice and the way he spoke was so cocky and aggressive, it sent chills up my spine. I think I was more hurt that they had the kids as a part of their plan. Even their behavior changed that day. I really didn't know what to do. I don't even remember what I said. I just wanted him out of my space. He basically gave me the rules on how things were about to go for now on. As soon as they left my room, I broke down in tears. Roommate number 2 and her baby's dad was trying to drain me for everything I had. How could I not see this coming?

So many things started to make sense. Her not having a second thought about leaving the kids. The fact that she said the kids lived with their dad but would only be with her on the weekends all added up. That only lasted shortly. They were there full time. I thought back to so many signs of roommate number 2 and her behavior. I was so consumed with covering up the lies, I hadn't been telling my audience that I allowed this woman to come into my life and turn it upside down. I had no idea what I was going to do. I had a man living in my house. I didn't know anything about him. The only thing I knew about him was what she told me about him. It was nothing good. She said one good thing about him and that was he took care of the girls. Everything else she told me was bad. She said he was very abusive and used to abuse her. She told me so many stories about him being with her. I cried so hard. I didn't know what to do or who to call. I couldn't believe what my life had become.

I moved to Vegas for a better life. I thought my situation with my ex-fiancé was the worst situation I had been in but it wasn't even close. I left one leach only to gain multiple leeches. I couldn't tell the difference. I was poor at judging people's characters. I continued to push away the people who were trying to help me only to end up in this situation. My little secrets that seemed like they could end me suddenly seemed so small. How had I gotten myself in this situation? I must have cried for hours as I listened to roommate number 2's family watch movies freely in my house. He was no longer hiding so he made sure to immediately make his presence known. I had no idea at the time that it was about to get really bad. This man would take me through things I could never imagine, and I would become a prisoner in my own home.

The first thing I did when I finally pulled myself together was call my landlord. I wanted to know if what he was saying was true. Was he considered a resident now? When my landlord told me that what he said was the truth and what I needed to do to get him out, I was overwhelmed. This was planned and I was clueless of what was going on. Roommate 2 and her baby's dad, the unwanted guest, had turned out to be professional Squatters. They would just take over people's homes. I was an easy target because I was becoming bed-ridden. The only times I would really ever leave the house was once a month when I did my club, and I would go to the salon when we had a special guest. Other than that, I worked from home, and I never left my room. I felt stupid because how could I not see something like this happening? How did I let my life and home get so out of control?

I was so shocked and overwhelmed after my landlord told me I would literally have to file an eviction to get this man out of my house. I couldn't help but break down and cry all over again. I would have to actually go through the court process to get this man, who I didn't know, out of my house. I could barely move around. How was I going to even start the procedures? I started calling around asking for help. I thought that if I wasn't able to get around that maybe I could start the court procedures from over the phone. They made it so hard for me that eventually I just gave up. It was just all too much for me. Instead of putting my foot down and getting out of the bed I did the unthinkable.

I talked myself into giving my unwanted guest a chance. What else could I do? She said that he was on disability, and he had a steady income. He also said he had been giving roommate number 2 rent money for months. I don't know how true this was because she was always late with her rent after the first couple months. Then before she went M. I. A., she hadn't paid anything. He could have been telling the truth because I was also paying her to work at the shop and she was still late with the rent until got smart and started to deduct the rent. Maybe she was lying. Just maybe, I could see how this is going to work out. I convinced myself that maybe he could be a good roommate. What other choice did I have? I had to make the best out of everything.

I had no idea how to break myself out of the slump I was in. I told myself I will give it a couple of days to see how things will go. Quickly, he turned my house into his house. He didn't do it slowly either. Things got really weird really fast. Remember the young lady I met at my BBW club night? Well, she kept in touch, and she was working for a nursing agency and had started to take care of me. He hated when I had company and he would always get the kids to spy on me or act like he was doing laundry so he could interrupt. He didn't say it at the time, but I started to feel like he was trying to put fear in me. It was as if he was warning me not to tell anyone he was a squatter turned unwanted roommate. He didn't have to try too hard. I was already scared of him. It was something about the way he looked. There was something very evil about his presence. I was nervous every time I had to converse with him, and I kept my bedroom door locked because I was just scared. I was in Vegas alone, away from my family, and they barely kept in touch. I didn't really have any friends left in Vegas because I kept everyone away from me. I didn't want them to know my life on line and my reality wasn't adding up. Roommate number 2 knew this, so I was an easy target.

As the weeks passed, I really started to feel like a visitor in my own home. I couldn't believe I didn't know he was there all that time because now he was loud. Maybe he could see the fear in my eyes every time I came in contact with him because he was no longer respecting my household. It was like it was a party every night. The loud music, drinking, and smoking was constant. I had to come up with a plan and I did what I always did. Threw myself into work.
If I was going to make a move, I had to get my finances in order. The salon was closed so I had to find a new location and

try to start over. I had to sell all my products. Roommate number 2 had stolen a lot of the lashes so all I really had was lipsticks, eyeshadows, and highlighters. You would think I was willing to sell everything I had to get me out of the bind, but that is not how I worked. That was also something I realized about myself when I had my manager.

When things started getting bad in the salon, she told me to sell some of my high end stuff. I collect luxury things. My head was in such a bad space, I refused to part ways with material things to get back on my feet. In my head, these material things made me. Although I'm still working on myself, just looking back at things like that, I became so ashamed of that situation because I refused to sell my LUXURY items. I decided to really work as many hours as I could from my work from home jobs. I was working from multiple jobs. I was at home and in my bed, but I put in the work. I needed a plan because things were getting worse by the day. I had an idea to do a photo shoot to sell my products and get some content for YouTube. It was normal for me to hold photoshoots at the house. The decor was gorgeous and over the top. The pool area was nice. Not as nice as before they moved in, but still nice enough.

They were supposed to stay in the guest house so there shouldn't be any reason they were even in the main part of the house, but they had started to feel entitled. He started to really believe in his head that this was his home. Also, I feel like he had started feeling like he had to keep an eye on who I spoke to and who was coming around. He couldn't let anyone in who was willing to help me. They played on the fact that I didn't have anyone, and my family never really checked on me. Every time I think about it, I want to kick myself. It was obvious that it was all planned out. I believe roommate number 2 ruined a lot of my relationships with my friends and employees so that I could be alone so that she and the unwanted guest could take advantage of me.

The day that I had the photo shoot, he came in and kept interrupting. The kids were running around. He was yelling and beating the kids. With one of the girls, he pulled her pants down in front of myself and my photographer and spanked her. It was a mess. My photographer was looking at me like what is going on in your house? But that's the thing: IT WAS NO LONGER MY HOUSE. I wanted to confide in my photographer and tell her I was scared. I wanted to ask for help but I felt like he was watching my every move. After that day, things started to get worse. He started to make sure I didn't have visitors. I had been working a lot during the night when things weren't as loud so during the day I tried to sleep. I didn't know until it was time for my nurse to come again that he had locked the gate. This man who wasn't supposed to be there in the first place had gone out and brought the biggest lock he could find to block anyone from coming to see me in my home. I was devastated. That was the last time anyone really came to see me. From then on, I was more or less just secluded in a house with a man that was daily becoming more and more disrespectful.

It got really bad when I told him I had decided I wanted to move. I had even spoken to my landlord to ask him if the unwanted guest could take over the lease. I thought this was a better solution than taking him to court. I mean they loved my house so much, they plotted and squatted all this time. Here was their chance to have the beautiful home I worked so hard to live in. They wanted my lifestyle, but they didn't want to sacrifice all that I had sacrificed to live the way I lived. I was tired anyway and to keep it real, I couldn't keep up with the lifestyle myself. Everything was falling apart. I was ok with downsizing at this point. I was about to pay all the bills while this stranger stayed at my house. I would have thought he would have been happy, but he wasn't. This is when the torture and disrespect really began. It was a pattern with him and roommate number two. The minute they realized I wasn't about to let them use me they turned into monsters.

He told me he was ok with the agreement of him taking over the lease, but he wasn't. He was more comfortable with being a squatter. He started locking the gate so none of my company could get in and walking around the house screaming and yelling at the top of his lungs. One day he banged on my bedroom door for a good 10 minutes calling me every name I could think of. You fat stinking bitch, he screamed, open this fucking door! He claimed that he wanted to use the washer and dryer and the laundry room was connected to my room. I was scared. This man had me so scared. In less than a few weeks of me finding out that he had been living there he had turned me into a prisoner of my own house. I had no one to call and I just knew that one day soon that he was going to kill me. I was completely bed-ridden by then so I couldn't just get up and leave.

It had been months since I spoke to my family. I had been secluding myself from the world because I was embarrassed by how big I had gotten and how the salon had failed. I was an easy target because by then no one was checking on me and it was my own fault. I had secluded myself from the world. Nobody was coming to save me from this crazy, unwanted, guest.

For weeks, I lived in fear. One day, he just snapped when I told him once again the landlord had called, and I had found another apartment. If he wanted the house, he had to pay the landlord and sign a sublease. He called me so many names and just started throwing my furniture out in the backyard. My beautiful custom-made furniture. That was just the beginning.

He began threatening my life and walking around the house with a gun like he was guarding it. He was holding me at gunpoint, and I became every bitch in the book. I was scared for my life. Not only was he extra aggressive with me he was extra aggressive with his kids. I was so scared that I even tried to reach out to roommate number 2 again. I became a prisoner in my own room. Every day I just planned my escape. If he wasn't going to take over the lease, I was going to have to break it because I was living in fear. I was bigger than I ever had been in my life. I could barely get around and roommate number 2 had moved her crazy baby father in my house and left me and her kids with him. I know you're thinking that this chapter alone sounds like a sitcom but it's true. I can't make this shit up but wait, it gets worse.

I was plotting my escape from the prison that once was my beautiful home. I was racking my brain thinking of who I could call to help me. Looking back at that time now gives me the shivers not just because of the crazy unwanted guest, but my mind frame. I was still trying to protect my image. It was a lot of people who I could have reached out to, but my pride wouldn't let me. I couldn't let anyone see how much I weighed. I needed to hide how big I gotten. I needed to hide the fact that the shop closed, and I was sitting in a house with a man who was threatening to kill me. I didn't reach out for help because I didn't want to expose myself. What was I thinking?

The fact that I'm still here to even tell this story is a miracle. Months passed and life was getting worse for me. I was getting low on food and the unwanted guest would lock the gate. It was hard for me to even order because the delivery guys couldn't get in the gate. I had to ask his permission to even get groceries delivered to my own house. At that point, I had no more fight left in me. I was so depressed I didn't care what happened. This one particular day, as soon as I woke up, I had an eerie feeling. I wasn't a real religious person, but I had started really praying for God to help me. I could feel something was about to happen, but I just didn't know what it was. I had so much anxiety. I was literally shaking like a leaf throughout the day. I hope he wasn't going to try to harm me, and I tried to stay as quiet as I could so him and the girls wouldn't bother me. I couldn't put my finger on what was going to happen, but I could feel that it was going to be bad.

As the day passed, the house was unusually quiet which only made me more nervous but still the day passed without anything bad happening. I drifted off to sleep and I was awakened by a loud noise. Yelling and screaming. Just like that, a bunch of men with guns were in my room. At first, I thought we were being robbed or they were coming to harm him for something he had done. I didn't know about who he was outside of the house, but I remembered hearing stories from roommate number 2 about his drug abuse. I didn't know what was going on and I was confined to my bed so I couldn't do anything but stare back at the men with guns in fear. I was relieved when they announced that they were the police. I knew I hadn't done anything wrong, so I knew they were there for him. Hearing the cries of his daughters in the other room broke my heart but I was relieved they were arresting him.

I still didn't know why right away, until the detective questioned me and told me they were there because he had raped our neighbor. I didn't really know the neighbors. I had maybe seen them once or twice but had never had a conversation with them. According to the detective he had asked the teenage neighbor to babysit his kids but forced himself on her and raped he. He raped a young girl under my roof with me and his daughters in the house. My mind began to race as the detective explained to me what was going on. I remembered the anxiety I felt the day before. I remember all the times he threatened me. I remember him telling me I better stop sleeping with my butt in the air around him. I remembered how afraid of him his daughters seemed. I had a devil under my roof. I was relieved when the police told him they were arresting him, but I was heartbroken that the Child Protective Service was taking the girls in their custody. I tried to get in touch with roommate number 2 to tell her that her kids were being placed in state custody, but she wouldn't respond.

I was already preparing to move but I had to get out of there quickly. I didn't know if he would get out on bail and come back. He had always told me that if I told anyone about him holding me at gunpoint, he would kill me. The detective had told me that the neighbor, the girl he raped, had told them he said he was planning to kill me. He told her I was a burden, and he was going to kill me. I didn't know how I survived that situation, but I did, and I had to get out of that house before he came back. I reached out to an old friend and let them know what was going on with me. In two weeks, I was completely moved out.

I was so scared, I made sure my next place was in a gated community. You would have thought after the horrible experience I just endured that I would get my life back on track. That was my intention. The first night I was safely in my new place I felt relieved. I had my life back and I had plans to get back on track. In my mind at the time, I thought the new environment would put me on my A game. I was tired and ready to lose the weight and also get my life back. Mentally, I was more screwed up than I admitted to myself. Within weeks, I was back to secluding myself and overeating. Things were really bad before they got good again.

Unhealthy Habits

I hadn't been to a doctor's appointment in years. The more I secluded myself the more I ate. I had gotten so big that my health was declining fast. I had to get out of bed because it was time for me to shoot my show. I was under contract, but they had no idea how big I was. It was bad enough I had lost the salon, which was a big part of the show, but I promised the producers I would have another salon soon. This particular day, I wanted them to come shoot in my new place. This was good for me because I could barely get around. My legs were leaking so much water and I didn't know it at the time, but my heart was failing. I was killing myself and didn't even know it. I was in denial. My only goal was getting my salon back open and not to focus on my health. I had been working overtime from home and I had saved enough money to rent another salon, but I was feeling horrible.

I had a girl reach out to me and we had been talking for a few months. I told her I was looking to hire a new stylist because I would be opening a new salon. She called me every day to help me, but she was all the way in Florida. I had been telling her that she could come to Las Vegas so we could get the new salon open, but I couldn't let her see how big I had gotten. I was really sick at this point, but still in denial. My mental health was just as bad as my physical health. I was so in denial. That day was the first time I went to the hospital, and I was in for a rude awakening about how sick I was but still in the back of my mind I was thinking about the salon. I stayed in the hospital for weeks. I probably would have been there longer, but the spread of Covid-19 had started.

This was the first time I saw my family in years. My mom, sister, and oldest brother had finally made it to Vegas to see me. It wasn't what I dreamed of. They weren't there because I had accomplished something. I couldn't get them to come when things were good and when I was on the morning show, or the mayor was at my ribbon cutting. Not even when my salon doors were open. They didn't show up to see my lavish gown or my amazing glam. I had been begging them for years to come see what I was building. If only I had my family around more than I wouldn't have been through most of the stuff I was going through. Instead of the excitement, I wanted to see their faces, I saw the disappointment. They weren't here because they wanted to be here, but they were here because some doctor called them. I remember the day I was brought home. The look on their faces while they helped me get in the hospital bed. My sister looked sad. My mom was ashamed, but it was the look of my oldest brother that I won't be able to shake. The look he had on his face when helping me get settled was a look of disgust. At that moment I was angry that they left my little brother behind. I knew no matter what, the look he gave me would have been the look of love and no judgment.

I was embarrassed but that didn't last long because they didn't stay long. Within a few days, I was back alone in my house. I know I already told y'all a little bit about that experience in the beginning of the book. I had to go back through it so you could know my mind frame at the time.

I met this young lady. She came into my life during a pandemic after all I had been through. She had no idea what she was walking into because on social media, I still had my audience thinking that my life was just fine. It wasn't like they were asking a lot of questions about the salon being closed; it was a pandemic. In my head I had time to get back on track. I just continued posting old pictures lying about how fabulous my life was. I quickly got back into my routine. I threw myself back into work. If I didn't work, then who was going to pay my bills. It damn sure wasn't going to be my family because I was the one, they came to. One of me on again off again boyfriends that I hadn't seen in almost a year never comes around when things are bad. He only comes around when the camera is about to roll. Through everything I had been through that year he wasn't there. It's not like I wanted him to see me at my worst. I kinda went M. I. A. on him too but i'm not going to make excuses for him. He knew how to get in touch with me when he needed to. It was time to get a lease and start planning for the new salon.

My new friend I had been talking to for the last few months about helping me reopen the salon was finally coming to see me. She was only supposed to be there for two days and ended up staying for months. The second day she was there she had to call the ambulance for me. She had no idea how sick I was because there I was on social media acting like everything was ok.

Pink Shoes

I've been through a lot in the last few years. Only a few people were there to save my life. The castmate, the young lady who came to town to find a job, ended up taking me back home with her to help take care of me. I sat in the back of a U-Haul on a mattress for days. I thought I was going to die, but she got me there and took care of me the best she could until my producers came to bring me back to Vegas to Prepare to start shooting the show. I would like to thank her. I've learned in the process of writing this book that I am harder on some of the women in my life. I get mad at them for little things like keeping my favorite pair of Gucci Glasses or telling a secret I only told them.

I want to apologize because there have been some women that came into my life to where that if it wouldn't have been for them, I don't know where I would be. I've also learned that I've been putting up with a lot of things from the men in my life letting them get away with things that

I wouldn't let the women who help me get away with. I'm quick to walk away from friendships but the relationships I should walk away from I tend to stay longer than I should. I met two guys when I got to Vegas. One abandoned me as soon as I got here when I wouldn't let him control my business. I dealt with him going to social media airing out all my business and I still kept him in my life.

Eventually, I cut him off but the other relationship I'm still in. It's toxic and I know he isn't with me for all the right reasons. He wasn't there for me for all the things I went through since I was in Vegas but when he needed me, he showed up. I don't want to really go into detail with this relationship because I'm still in it. I know I said I was going to be completely honest in the beginning of this book so here it is: I'm still battling when it comes to relationships with men. This man has told me many times that he wasn't attracted to me, and I still won't break it off. I know he's only with me for some of the opportunities I have provided, and I know that sooner than later things will end. At this point, I'm just trying to get the strength to walk away. I've been alone for so long that I'm just settling to just have him around. I know that he has a life without me, and he may be in another relationship but for some reason I keep dealing with him.

I know that also he just knows because we are in production and as soon as the cameras start rolling that I won't see him again until he needs me, or I have an opportunity for him. I don't know why this even makes me feel so sad when I think of it. I know he doesn't love me the way I love him. I'm not going to go in detail about our relationship right now. That is going to have to be in book number 2. I can't pretend that I don't know my fate with this man. I can pretend that I won't keep putting up with his bullshit. I don't know if I will walk away or if I will try to fix it. There Is still a lot I have to work on. Once I learn to love myself more then maybe I will make better choices in men.

Throughout this book and my life period men have been my downfall. That's no secret. I can promise you Dolls that I'm working on myself every day. Although I lost a lot of weight, I still have things mentally and emotionally that I have to deal with. Be patient with me and keep me in your prayers as I walk into the next stage of my life. Notice I said walk! These days I'm walking again. The hardest thing I ever had to do was learn how to walk again. Remember, I had been bed bound and fighting for my life for 2 years. Imagine not using your leg muscles for that long. Yes, I lost a lot of weight, but I still was scared to walk. I was terrified of falling. I fell once before, and it was the most terrifying thing ever.

Throughout the journey of me trying to walk again, I had to find the right shoes. I found a pair of Pink Nikes. If you know me, then you know that sneakers weren't my first choice. It's no secret I'm a fancy girl who likes over the top things. I love heels and slides. It's been a long time since I could get around in heels. If you saw me in a pair, I was sitting down. Most likely I took them off as soon as I took a picture of them. The last few years, I couldn't even fit my feet in a pair of heels. The sneakers that I picked were cute and stylish because that's who I am. It was something more about these shoes than them being cute. They made me feel safe and secure. I knew these shoes were going to help me change my life and walk again. I almost feel like these shoes had special powers. They made me feel like I could do it.

I took my first couple of steps with these sneakers, and I have been walking ever since. I remember how painful it used to be to just take a few steps. At one point it was a lot to just stand up. A couple of days a week I had to have a physical therapist come out to work my legs. I knew I wanted to walk again, and I would dream of myself running on the beach, but I can't say I didn't use every excuse to not do the therapy. My physical therapist would push me in my cute pink shoes. Nowadays, I can walk again. I still have trouble getting around so I'm still in therapy. The other day while in the new salon I heard one of the girls talking about how I keep wearing these same pink shoes. She couldn't understand why I looked so fabulous but when you got down to my shoes every day, I wore the same pink Nike's. At first, I was offended. I wanted to curse her out. I was upset for the remainder of the day. When I got home, I called a friend and she said something to me that stuck with me. I didn't have to explain to anyone what my pink shoes meant to me.

Without knowing, I had made them my security blanket and it was up to me when I was ready to let them go. I will always love my pretty pink Nike's and it will be a while before I completely get rid of them. They brought me out of my storm. It's time to get a new pair of shoes but every chance I get I will get stronger, and my pink shoes will forever remind me of how I stepped into the next chapter of my life. I'm not perfect Dolls, but every

day I will become a better version of
myself. The end and new beginning.

First time standing on my own after surgery

Salon Opening Day

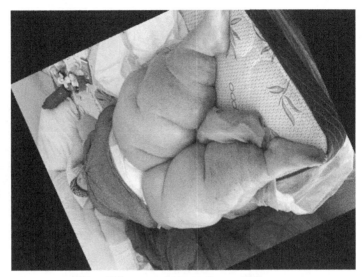

The Worse time of my life

Weight Loss Journey